HISTORIC PHOTOS OF
STEAMBOATS
ON THE MISSISSIPPI

TEXT AND CAPTIONS BY DEAN M. SHAPIRO

TURNER
PUBLISHING COMPANY

Crowds gather for President's Day on the St. Louis riverfront in 1907, celebrating the arrival of
President Theodore Roosevelt aboard the steamer *Mississippi*. The Eads Bridge is in the background.

HISTORIC PHOTOS OF
STEAMBOATS
ON THE MISSISSIPPI

Turner Publishing Company
4507 Charlotte Avenue • Suite 100
Nashville, Tennessee 37209
(615) 255-2665

www.turnerpublishing.com

Historic Photos of Steamboats on the Mississippi

Library of Congress Control Number: 2009922628

ISBN: 978-1-59652-542-9

ISBN: 978-1-68442-094-0 (hc)

Printed in the United States of America

09 10 11 12 13 14 15 16—0 9 8 7 6 5 4 3 2 1

CONTENTS

Four side-wheelers tie up at the New Orleans docks in the late 1850s to take on cargo, mainly cotton, as seen in the left foreground. From right to left they are the *Colonel T. H. Judson,* the *Lecompte,* the *Milton Relf,* and an unidentifiable steamboat. All three of the identifiable packets were homeported in the South and were pressed into service by the Confederacy.

ACKNOWLEDGMENTS

This volume, *Historic Photos of Steamboats on the Mississippi,* is the result of the cooperation and efforts of many individuals, organizations, and corporations. It is with great thanks that we acknowledge the valuable contribution of the Library of Congress for its generous support.

The author wishes to express his gratitude to the following organizations and individuals for their valuable assistance in bringing this book to fruition:

The University of Wisconsin-La Crosse for the photos that originated from their extensive steamboat archive;
The Jefferson Parish Public Library for their assistance in locating the books consulted for this work;
Michael McCalip of Turner Publishing Company for his guidance, assistance, and expertise in moving this book along toward completion and publication;
and especially my daughter, Heather, for her assistance with writing the towboat captions and the glossary, and my son, Jonathan, for upgrading my computer which allowed me to work faster and more efficiently.

———————

With the exception of touching up imperfections that have accrued with the passage of time and cropping where necessary, no changes have been made to the photographs. The focus and clarity of many photographs is limited by the technology and the ability of the photographer at the time they were taken.

PREFACE: THE ROMANCE OF STEAMBOATING

"When I was a boy, there was but one permanent ambition among my comrades in our village on the west bank of the Mississippi River. That was, to be a steamboatman. We had transient ambitions of other sorts, but they were only transient. . . . These ambitions faded out, each in its turn; but the ambition to be a steamboatman always remained."
—Chapter 4, *Life on the Mississippi* by Mark Twain (1883)

No nation in history has ever had a more passionate love affair with its primary means of transportation than the United States of America. Throughout our long existence, we have been enamored of our horses, our railroads, and our automobiles. So much so, in fact, that we composed songs and wrote books and flowery odes extolling the conveyances that got us from Point A to Point B and everywhere in between. To this list, we must add our steamboats.

For nearly a century and a half, steamboats were the primary means of conveyance for large numbers of people along our navigable waterways. Long before railroads and superhighways, human and freight traffic moved on our rivers, transported by the miracle of steam power—often hundreds or thousands of miles. During the late 1800s, the steamboat was a key contributor to our westward expansion and growth.

At the epicenter of this vast waterborne transport network was the Mississippi River. The longest river in North America and one of the most heavily traveled in the world, "Old Man River," as it is fondly known in song and folklore, is the dividing line of the continent. With tributaries flowing into it from the east and the west, the Mississippi River is the trunk line for a watershed that drains 1,245,000 square miles and comprises nearly 10,000 miles of navigable water. During most of the nineteenth century and nearly half of the twentieth, the steamboat reigned supreme along the Mississippi and its many tributaries, serving the major river port cities of America's heartland.

With their paddle wheels churning, their tall smokestacks billowing, their calliopes singing, and their steam whistles sounding, the proud steamboats that plied the Mighty Mississippi and the rivers that fed into it were deeply ingrained into the national culture and consciousness. They carried cotton, sugar, wood products, produce, and other raw materials from port to port. They towed logs to sawmills to be made into lumber. They transported people between cities and towns long before they were connected by overland routes. They delivered mail and brought news—both good and bad—to denizens of a region far removed from where major events were happening.

Steamboats brought entertainment to many people and to many places they stopped at along the way. They nurtured the early careers of some of our nation's musical pioneers. They carried many of the giants of our nation's literary, social, and political cultures, including writers like Walt Whitman and Mark Twain, who literally took his *nom de plume* from the steamboat lexicon ("two fathoms deep"). Presidents and foreign dignitaries rode the Mississippi's currents, visiting storied riparian locales that made up the great tapestry of the still-developing American nation.

However, steamboating was also fraught with danger. Boilers that got too hot could explode. Burning cinders escaping through smokestacks or a carelessly discarded cigar could fall on a bale of cotton and quickly set a boat ablaze. Hidden snags just below a river's waterline could impale a steamboat and tear a nasty hole in a wooden hull. Expanding ice pressing against a wood hull could crush it, while huge chunks of floating ice could push moored boats into each other or against overhead structure supports. A collision with another vessel or a bridge support could spell disaster for a boat, its crew, and its passengers. Storms that came up suddenly, especially tornadoes, could cause a fragile craft to founder. During droughts that lowered water levels, boats could run aground on hidden sandbars. A steamboat on the Mississippi River and its tributaries faced many navigational hazards, both natural and man-made, and any of these calamities could result in losses of lives and valuable cargo. In fact, the average lifespan of a steamboat in the nineteenth century was six to seven years.

But despite the hazards, steamboating retained and still retains its romantic charm. The splash of the paddle wheel in the water has a calming effect on the soul as the scenery passes slowly by. Many a contemplative moment was spent on many a deck by those traversing the waterways, content to go at their own pace—a pace much slower than today's automobiles traveling at 80 miles per hour or airplanes traveling at several hundred.

The photographs in this book that follow capture the magic of this glorious era that continues even to the present day.

—*Dean M. Shapiro*

The Union gunboat *Signal* rests alongside lumber-carrying barges, most likely on the Red River. Built in Wheeling in 1862, it was sold to the U.S. Navy later that year and converted into a tinclad at the start of the Civil War. The *Signal* was captured by the Confederates on the Red River in Louisiana on May 5, 1864.

Introduction: The Early Years of Steamboating

(1780–1859)

Based on the design from Scotsman James Watt's 1769 steam engine, John Fitch designed and built the first crude steamboats 20 years later, running them on the Delaware River. In 1807, Robert Fulton ran his side-wheeler, *Clermont,* up the Hudson River from New York to Albany in 32 hours at five miles an hour. This milestone ushered in the Steamboat Era.

In 1811, the *New Orleans,* built from a design by Fulton and Robert Livingston, became the first steamboat to successfully travel down the Mississippi to New Orleans. It was piloted by Captain Nicholas Roosevelt, an ancestor of the two American presidents. The journey was an adventure in more ways than one. An earthquake, believed to be the largest ever reported in America, struck around New Madrid, Missouri, hampering the boat's passage and actually changing the course of the river near the quake's epicenter. The crew's arrival in New Orleans on January 10, 1812, was a major triumph of technology.

By 1814, Fulton and Edward Livingston (brother of Robert Livingston) were offering regular passenger and freight steamboat service between New Orleans and Natchez, Mississippi. Their boats traveled at the rates of eight miles per hour downstream and three miles per hour upstream. However, significant adjustments had to be made to Mississippi River steamboats to render them more practical and efficient.

The task of redesign fell to Henry Shreve, who noted that the rounded, deep-draft hulls of the Fulton steamboats may have worked well on deep, slow-moving Eastern rivers but not in shallower, faster waters like those of the Mississippi and its tributaries. Shreve designed a steamboat with a flat, shallow hull that could float in as little as two or three feet of water, and this revolutionized river travel on the western waterways. He was also instrumental in designing the first snagboats that could remove subsurface hazards and break up logjams. Shreveport, Louisiana, on the Red River, was named in his honor.

Following Shreve's designs, river traffic flourished in the first half of the nineteenth century along the Mississippi and the rivers that fed into it, primarily the Ohio and Missouri rivers and their tributaries. Cities and towns along the rivers capitalized on river trade. Settlements in the West, some of which grew into major cities like Kansas City and Omaha, owe much of their early development to the steamboat. Everywhere these boats traveled, they brought life and commerce vital to the survival of remote outposts that had no other transportation link with the rest of the nation.

Steamboats bore the names of their home port cities and individuals associated with them, especially female members of boat-owning families. In their prime, some boats became "floating palaces" with all the comforts of home—and more!

The Civil War, Reconstruction, and the Resumption of River Commerce

(1860-1879)

Over the years, steamboat design continued to evolve. The earliest side-wheelers had paddles on each side of the boat; then came stern-wheelers with one huge wheel at the rear of the vessel in the 1850s. High-pressure engines were devised that could power a boat more easily through strong currents.

Prior to the 1860s, packet steamboats were the primary means of conveyance for people and freight all along the navigable lengths of the Mississippi and its major tributaries. Operating from Henry Shreve's design for shallow-draft vessels, hundreds of steamboats traveled thousands of miles, delivering passengers and goods to remote locations as well as major river port cities.

In the early 1860s, however, as hostilities between the northern and southern sections of the United States erupted into the Civil War, waterborne commerce below the Ohio River came to a virtual standstill. Secessionist and sympathetic border states controlled the lower section of the Mississippi between 1861 and mid-1863. Packet boats were conscripted for wartime use by both North and South. Some were used for troop and war materiel transport; others were armored with iron plates and retrofitted with deck guns for assault on riparian strongholds and enemy gunboats. With the capture of Vicksburg, Mississippi, by the Union Army in July 1863, the full length of the Mississippi was in Union hands, and steamboat commerce resumed to a limited extent.

During Reconstruction and the years immediately afterward, packet steamboats reasserted the importance they had during the pre-war years, once again delivering passengers and freight to their destinations. New Orleans, which was largely unscathed by the hostilities, flourished as a major shipping hub for the cotton trade and other raw and finished products. Other cities in the Mississippi River system flourished also, especially as steamboat technology advanced.

The 1870s saw a tremendous boom in steamboat construction, with the shipbuilding yards at Brownsville, Pennsylvania, turning out hundreds of boats, thanks to its proximity to Pittsburgh, where most boat engines were being built. The yards at Jeffersonville, Indiana, across the Ohio River from Louisville, also contributed their share of riverboats to the existing registry. By the end of that decade, steamboats were poised on the threshold of their greatest era.

The *Aleck Scott*, a packet built in 1848 in Louisville and St. Louis, ran between St. Louis and New Orleans in the 1850s. One of its pilots was Captain Horace Bixby, who was accompanied by the famous writer Mark Twain. In this photo, the *Scott* picks up Union troops at Cairo, Illinois, in 1862 for battle at Fort Henry on the Tennessee River. Later that year it was commissioned as a gunboat and renamed *Lafayette*.

The *Federal Arch* (center) unloads cargo to waiting horse teams and dockworkers on the wharf at Keokuk, Iowa. A side-wheeler that made the Ohio River–Mississippi River run between Pittsburgh and St. Louis, the *Federal Arch* had a short life. Built in 1850, it was destroyed by ice and the impact of another boat being pushed into it while being dismantled in St. Louis in February 1856.

Advertisement for the *Golden Era*, a side-wheeler built in Wheeling, Virginia (now West Virginia), in 1852. It made port calls at river towns in Illinois and Iowa and as far upriver as Minnesota. During the Civil War, it transported Union troops as far south as Vicksburg. After several sales to New Orleans–based captains in the mid-1860s, it was dismantled in 1868.

In November 1864, Union troops led by General John A. Logan board the side-wheel packet ship *Des Moines* in Vicksburg for a southbound journey to the Red River. Like many other packet steamboats during the Civil War, the *Des Moines* was pressed into service to transport Union soldiers up and down the Ohio, Tennessee, and Mississippi rivers. The *Emerald*, another side-wheel packet used for troop transport, is in the background.

Advertisement for the *Dr. Kane*, a side-wheeler that made tramp runs on the Ohio and Mississippi rivers carrying passengers and freight between Pittsburgh, St. Louis, and St. Paul. An unusually large boat for the time, *Dr. Kane* weighed 191 tons. At the beginning of the Civil War, it transported Union troops into battle. However, it snagged and sank in deep water near Cairo, Illinois, in early March 1862.

The U.S. Navy gunboat *Brown* from the Mississippi River Fleet patrolled the river during the Civil War.

The U.S. Navy side-wheeler gunboat *Fort Hindman* was another ship in the navy's Mississippi River Fleet during the Civil War. Built in 1861, it was originally a ferry named *James Thompson* that operated on the Ohio River at Jeffersonville, Indiana. During the war, it was converted into a tinclad commanded by Captain James Pierce, and it carried nine guns. Dismantled after the war, its engines went into other ferries operating from Jeffersonville.

The *Tennessee* was a U.S. Navy gunboat in the Mississippi River Fleet. Originally named the *Exchange,* it was renamed in September 1865 after the Civil War ended. Converted to civilian commerce, it operated as a low-water boat between Evansville and Cairo in the late 1860s and made a trip up the Missouri River in the spring of 1869. It was wrecked on a snag at Louisville Bend near Decatur, Nebraska, on April 25.

An unidentified steamboat docks below the bluffs in Natchez, Mississippi, around 1864.

The overcrowded side-wheeler *Sultana* at Helena, Arkansas, in late April 1865. Among its nearly 2,000 passengers, many of whom are seen on the upper decks, were 1,880 Union soldiers returning home from the Civil War. On April 27, a faulty boiler caused three of the four boilers to explode, and the ship caught fire and sank seven miles above Memphis. Approximately 1,547 people were killed, 1,100 of whom were soldiers. It was the worst maritime disaster in American history.

Pictured is the eighth of ten steamboats named *Grey Eagle*, all built and operated between 1840 and 1918. This 70-ton side-wheeler, built in 1865, primarily ran the Mississippi River packet route between Keokuk, Iowa, and Quincy, Illinois, then moved up the Illinois River and ran between Peoria and Henry, Illinois. It sank at Henry in 1888.

The stern-wheel packet *Deer Lodge* in the Missouri River. Built in 1865 and designed specifically for the shallower waters of the Missouri, the ship made regular runs between St. Louis and Fort Benton, Montana, a distance of more than 3,000 miles. The *Deer Lodge* had its own onboard sawmill to cut wood for the boilers. It sank near St. Joseph, Missouri, in late 1865 and was raised and repaired, continuing in service until 1872.

The *Colorado* (left) and the *Denver* take on and discharge passengers at Omaha, Nebraska, on October 22, 1866. The two sister ships plied the Missouri River mainly between St. Joseph and Omaha, but occasionally ran as far upriver as the Yellowstone River in Montana. The *Colorado* sank in 1879, was raised and restored, and finally burned in St. Louis in 1884. The *Denver* burned in St. Joseph in 1867.

From left to right are the side-wheelers *Cornelia, Henry Ames,* and *Lizzie Gill* at the docks in New Orleans. The *Cornelia,* which made regular packet runs to and from New Orleans, burned in Algiers, Louisiana, in 1870. The *Henry Ames* ran between New Orleans and St. Louis. It sank after being snagged at Waterproof, Louisiana, in 1874, and two passengers drowned. The *Lizzie Gill* sank at the mouth of the White River in 1866, carrying a full cargo load.

Passengers aboard the packet stern-wheeler *G. B. Knapp* relax while the boat puts ashore at Taylors Falls, Minnesota, along the St. Croix River. Designed for the shallow waters of the tributaries of the upper Mississippi, the *Knapp* made runs between St. Paul and the small towns along the St. Croix and Minnesota rivers. After more than 20 years of service, it was dismantled in Stillwater, Minnesota, in 1889.

Built in 1864, the *Commonwealth* ran primarily between New Orleans and St. Louis, sometimes going up as far as Cincinnati. A side-wheel packet, it went through a series of owners during its 25-year lifespan and had smokestacks so high they had to be lowered to clear the suspension bridge across the Ohio River at Cincinnati. It burned there on August 25, 1889.

One of the few steamboats to enjoy a relatively long life, the side-wheel packet *Frank Pargoud* docks along the Mississippi in this 1870s photo. Named for a wealthy planter along the Ouachita River, the *Pargoud* lasted 15 years without any documented accidents. It transported passengers and cotton between New Orleans and Vicksburg, Greenville, Memphis, and smaller towns along the Ouachita. The boat's only captain, John Tobin, retired the *Pargoud* after replacing it with another packet in 1883.

The stern-wheel packet *George W. Wylly* paddles along on the Mississippi River carrying bales of cotton and a few passengers (ca. 1870). It was originally built to traverse the Flint River in Georgia, but little else is known about it. There is no listing for it in *Way's Packet Directory*.

In this photograph taken around 1870, passengers aboard the side-wheel packet *Alex Mitchell* are waiting to be seated before dining, in accordance with the custom of that time. Owned by a railroad conglomerate, the *Alex Mitchell* ran on the Ohio and upper Mississippi rivers, although it was reported to have made several runs between New Orleans and Shreveport along the Red River. Following several mishaps, it was dismantled in 1881.

The *Addie Johnston* docks along the upper Mississippi to take on cargo and passengers. A 315-ton, wood-hulled stern-wheel packet, the *Addie Johnston* was owned by several railroad companies and home-based in La Crosse, Wisconsin. It made runs upriver as far as St. Paul and along the St. Croix and Black rivers before being taken out of service in 1882.

Deckhands from the stern-wheel rafter/towboat *Abner Gile* labor at dockside in this 1870s photo. Homeported at La Crosse, the *Gile* enjoyed a 40-year run on the upper Mississippi under a succession of owners, including the boat's namesake from Clinton, Iowa. It was taken off the registry in 1912.

One of the largest and most opulently appointed side-wheel packets operating on the Mississippi was the *Great Republic,* shown here moored along the Mississippi. It had 54 staterooms and 10 more in the texas (upper) deck. Its maiden voyage from Pittsburgh in March 1867 brought out sightseers all along the Ohio River. However, bad management bankrupted the original owners after two years, and in the early 1870s, the boat was sold, rebuilt, and renamed the *Grand Republic.*

Interior of the *Great Republic,* displaying the opulent bar and overhead lighting. Once in service, the boat carried passengers and freight between St. Louis and New Orleans.

The *Alex Mitchell* docked at an unspecified location. Built in Paducah, Kentucky, and La Crosse in 1870, it was named for a president of the Milwaukee & St. Louis Railroad, with whom the boat's owners had been doing business. It had a run of bad luck, being frozen in ice at La Crosse, which caused hull damage, and wrecked by a tornado in 1876. It was dismantled in 1881, and its machinery went to the second *Gem City*.

Loaded up with hundreds of cotton bales, the exterior of the stern-wheel packet *Era No. 10* can barely be seen from the dock at Baton Rouge, Louisiana. Before it was a year old, *Era No. 10* collided with sister ship *Era No. 9* and sank at the mouth of the Red River in December 1868. Raised and salvaged, the ship lasted another 24 years before burning on the Boeuf River in Rayville, Louisiana.

With the help of workboats on the Mississippi River, the Eads Bridge between St. Louis, Missouri, and East St. Louis, Illinois, nears completion in 1874. The triple-span, ribbed steel arch bridge was more than a mile long with a clearance of 50 feet above high water. This engineering marvel was designed and built by Captain James B. Eads (1820–1887), who later designed the jetties at the mouth of the Mississippi that vastly improved river travel.

Named for a popular river news reporter from the *Cincinnati Commercial*, the stern-wheel packet *Cons Millar* is seen here loading barrels at an unspecified location. Little is documented about the boat other than its dimensions, owners, and various crews. It was built in Cincinnati in 1875 and plied the Ohio River, being seen in Paducah in December 1883. Its final fate was not recorded.

Crowds greet the side-wheel "cottonstyle" packet *Ed Richardson* as it arrives at its mooring place along the Mississippi in New Orleans. Its 1879 maiden voyage from Louisville to New Orleans was a memorable occasion for members of the wealthy Howard and Richardson cotton growing and brokering families. The boat served the Richardson cotton plantations and cottonseed oil company near Greenville, Mississippi, before being dismantled in 1888.

The Gilded Age: Western Settlement and Steamboats at the Height of Their Glory

(1880–1899)

By the start of the 1880s, steamboats were reaching the peak of their popularity and their highest figures in terms of passenger ridership and tonnage handled. With the opening of the American West for settlement, steamboats originating in St. Louis and other river ports on the upper Mississippi began transporting passengers and freight up the Missouri River and other western tributaries in record numbers. For settlements like Bismarck, North Dakota, Fort Benton, Montana, and other remote outposts on the edge of the western frontier, steamboats represented their lifelines to the rest of the nation before railroads arrived.

During the Reconstruction Era, railroads were booming and their lines eventually stretched out to the Pacific coast. Serious, sometimes hostile, competition broke out between steamboat and railroad companies with each touting its advantages, but during this time period, steamboats held their own. Though not able to go to landlocked locales and make deliveries like the railroads could, steamboats could deliver their goods and passengers to river ports cheaper than their competitors. Some railroad companies even built their own fleets of steamboats, so they had the best of both worlds. Steamboats they owned could carry goods to places the railroads hadn't yet serviced, as well as ferry train cars across wide, unbridged rivers like the Mississippi.

During this Golden Age, steamboats and their offerings became more lavish. Boats like the *J. M. White* and those built in Jeffersonville for the storied Anchor Line fleet were "floating palaces," featuring ornate decorative woodwork, luxurious suites and staterooms, plush chairs, gourmet meals, elaborate staircases, and even grand pianos—in short, all the amenities a well-to-do clientele could ever hope for. Prominent families like the Streckfus family of St. Louis and the Greenes of Cincinnati bought into the business, operating numerous riverboats simultaneously.

Steamboat racing, begun with the celebrated contest between the *Robert E. Lee* and the *Natchez* in 1870, grew in popularity as a spectator sport. Towboats, the less glamorous workhorses of the river, multiplied as the demand for the services they provided increased. Composite hulls of both iron (or steel) and wood were developed, making steamboat hulls less vulnerable to snags and jagged ice floes. This was the start of the modern era of safer, more sturdy all-steel hulls.

Eight identifiable steamboats crowd the waterfront in Vicksburg, Mississippi, in this 1883 photo. In numbered order they are (1) *Will S. Hays,* (2) *Ed Richardson,* (3) *Clara S.,* (4) *Deer Creek,* (5) the ferryboat *Anglia,* (6) *Helen Mead,* (7) *Sallie Carney,* (8) unnamed citizens' wharfboat, and (9) *Le Flore.* Strategically situated on the Mississippi at the mouth of the Yazoo River, Vicksburg was a key river port until a major course change in the late 1800s nearly left it high and dry.

Barrels line the dock at Sugar Landing, St. Louis, while (from left to right) the *Grover Cleveland, Assumption, Belle of the Coast, Clinton,* and *Warren* are moored there in this mid-1880s photo. The *Clinton,* built in 1872, ran the upper river and later between New Orleans and Bayou Sara, Louisiana. The *Assumption, Grover Cleveland* (named for the newly elected president in 1884), *Belle of the Coast,* and *Warren* also ran from New Orleans to smaller bayou outposts.

An interior view of the *Ed Richardson* shows the long parlor with tables and chairs, elaborate chandeliers, and other opulent furnishings and décor.

The side-wheel packet *Dean Adams* loads cotton at a wharf along the Mississippi. In operation for only about six years, it ran primarily between Vicksburg and Arkansas City on the Arkansas River. After the *Idlewild* burned, it ran between Arkansas City and Memphis, and it, too, burned at a Memphis wharf in 1886.

A group of boys swim around and play on log rafts being towed by the *F. C. A. Denkmann*. A stern-wheel rafter, the *Denkmann* was built in Dubuque in 1881 and once brought a raft to Rock Island that was 1,625 feet long and 275 feet wide. It was the largest raft to come down the Mississippi. In October 1899, it was used to tow corn along the Wabash River in Indiana to Nashville, and it was renamed the *Wabash* that same year.

The *Edward J. Gay* takes on cargo along the Mississippi. A side-wheel packet, it ran primarily between New Orleans and Bayou Sara, carrying passengers, cargo, and U.S. mail. It was the second steamboat with that name, replacing one that burned on the Yalobusha River in Mississippi during the Civil War. It also burned, in 1888, at the First Street Wharf in New Orleans.

In this souvenir photo, the rafter-packet *Eclipse* takes on passengers at Cassville, Wisconsin. It was the ninth of eleven steamboats bearing the name between 1842 and 1917. Built in LeClaire, Iowa, in 1882, it ran mostly on the upper Mississippi between Dubuque, Iowa, and Prairie du Chien, Wisconsin. However, its last voyage was on the Ohio River in late 1917, when it struck a dike at the foot of Neville Island and burned and sank.

Horse-drawn dray wagons line up to pick up cargo from the *Edward J. Gay* along the Mississippi. It was built in Cincinnati in 1878, and its roof bell came from the *Brilliant,* which was taken out of service around 1850.

A group of passengers gamble aboard the *Dora* as wait staff looks on. A stern-wheel packet built in Metropolis, Illinois, in 1880, the *Dora* ran from St. Louis up the Illinois River, then later between St. Louis and Clarksville, Missouri. *Way's Packet Directory* says it sank about ten miles above St. Louis in December 1894, while another account says it was dismantled in St. Louis in 1895.

Passengers look ashore as the *Golden Gate* lies moored along the Ohio River at Louisville, Kentucky. A stern-wheel packet built in 1878, it ran mostly on the upper Mississippi between Hannibal and St. Louis, and later on the Illinois and Ohio rivers. By the early 1900s, it was running on the Kentucky River and was dismantled at Carrollton, Kentucky, in 1903.

Crew members of the *Gem City* come ashore along the Mississippi. A side-wheel packet, it ran between St. Louis and Keokuk, Iowa. It was bought out by the Diamond Jo Line in 1891 and rebuilt as the *Quincy* at Dubuque in 1895.

The stern-wheel packet *E. W. Cole* is tied up on the New Orleans waterfront between an unidentified boat on the left and another unidentified boat (possibly the *Columbia*) on the right. The *Cole* originally ran between Memphis and Vicksburg, then ran from New Orleans up Bayou Lafourche. On New Year's Day 1891, it hit a snag at Welham's Landing on the Mississippi and was lost.

The ornate interior parlor in the *City of Vicksburg*. The second of two side-wheel packets bearing the name, this version had five large boilers and two paddles measuring 33 feet in diameter. It was built in Jeffersonville, Indiana, in 1881 and was seriously damaged by a tornado at St. Louis in 1896. Two years later it was sold to a New Orleans company and rebuilt as the *Chalmette*.

Crew and passengers look out from the upper and lower decks of the moored stern-wheel rafter *Abner Gile* in this 1880s photo. It was built in 1872 and was used in rafting on the upper Mississippi, dropping logs out from St. Paul, Minnesota, to Prescott, Wisconsin, at the mouth of the St. Croix River. It was inspected at Galena, Illinois, in 1877 and ran until it wore out in 1912.

In this undated photo, five fashionably dressed women pose on deck of the *City of Winona* in front of the pilothouse. Built in Dubuque in 1882, this stern-wheel packet was originally a rafter towing logs to the sawmill of its owners in Winona, Minnesota. It was later bought by Captain John Streckfus of the famous Streckfus riverboat family to compete in the Davenport-Clinton, Iowa, trade. Rebuilt in the early 1890s, it was renamed *Winona*.

Passengers aboard the *City of Winona* sit down to dinner in a private parlor. As was customary for the time, the women sat opposite the men, and all of them were dressed in formals for dinner.

The side-wheel packet *City of St. Louis* is moored at dockside in New Orleans in this 1891 photo. The first of three ships bearing the name, it was built in 1883 and made runs between its namesake city and New Orleans during its 20-year lifespan. President William McKinley was a passenger in May 1901, just four months before his assassination. While laid up at Carondelet, Missouri, the boat burned on October 29, 1903.

The *Natchez* (left), the *Garland* (center), and an unidentified steamboat at right are moored at a busy dock, probably in New Orleans. The *Garland*, a stern-wheel packet built in 1888, was homeported in New Orleans and sank in or around 1893 just below St. Maurice, Louisiana. The *Natchez* shown here is the tenth of twelve steamboats to bear the name, the most recent of which still operates in New Orleans as a stern-wheeler, carrying sightseers and Dixieland bands.

The side-wheel packet *Grey Eagle* takes on cargo at an unspecified location. Built in 1892, its home port was St. Louis, and it operated between there and Cape Girardeau and Vicksburg. The last in a line of ten *Grey Eagle*s dating back to 1840, this one participated in riverborne festivities for presidents Theodore Roosevelt in 1907 and William Howard Taft in 1909. It was destroyed by ice on the Ohio River at Paducah in January 1918.

An unidentified woman holds a baby and escorts two children up the gangplank onto the *Eloise* in this photo taken around 1900. Originally built in 1889 as a stern-wheel towboat named *Eliza H.*, it was converted into a packet in 1898. Running between Keokuk and Burlington, Iowa, it sank in shallow water at Pontoosuc, Illinois, and, after being raised, it burned at Keokuk. Sold in 1907, it was restored and renamed *Wenona*.

Passengers aboard the *Dubuque* enjoy their privacy in the boat's modest parlor. The third of three boats bearing the name of the Iowa River port city, the *Dubuque* was built in 1879 and originally named the *Pittsburgh*. After losing its upper deck to a tornado at St. Louis in 1896, the boat's hull was repaired in Dubuque, and the boat was renamed. It ran primarily on the upper Mississippi for 40 years.

From left to right, the *Ferd Herold, J. N. Harbin,* and *Kate Adams* take on cargo at the Memphis wharf in the 1890s. The *Ferd Herold,* a stern-wheel packet named after a St. Louis brewer who financed construction, ran the mid-Mississippi, docking at points between Vicksburg and Alton, Illinois. The *J. N. Harbin* was also a stern-wheel packet running the mid-Mississippi and Ouachita river routes. The second of three boats named *Kate Adams* ran between Memphis and Arkansas City.

The stern-wheel packet *City of Quincy* takes on passengers and freight on the Mississippi. Built in its namesake city in 1891, it ran to Keokuk and later to St. Louis. In March 1896, it was sold to the wealthy Parmalee family of St. Louis and converted into a pleasure boat. However, two months later it was destroyed by a tornado at St. Louis that sank or seriously damaged 14 other vessels moored there at the time.

The stern-wheel rafter *E. Rutledge* and a barge it is towing are docked along the Mississippi at Winona, Minnesota, in this 1890s photo. Owned by the Rock Island Lumber Company, the *E. Rutledge* was built in 1881 and once brought a raft to Rock Island that was 1,430 feet long and 285 feet wide. After its rafting days, its home port changed to St. Paul in 1909, and it was renamed *John H. Rich* in 1910.

The stern-wheel packet *A. L. Mason* had a very short life running the Missouri River between St. Louis and Kansas City and the Mississippi between St. Louis and New Orleans. Built in 1890, the boat was carrying a heavy load down the Mississippi in June 1894 when it sank off Sunflower Landing. One of the boat's hogchains, an adjustable steel cable that helped support the weight of the paddle wheel and other structures, snapped, causing the vessel to go down.

Wait staff members stand in place awaiting the arrival of diners aboard the *City of St. Louis*. Serving dinner and cleaning rooms were among the few jobs open to African-Americans aboard steamboats at that time. The device on the right at the front of the picture dispensed fresh water, which had to be carried aboard during most steamboat journeys.

Passengers disembark from the *City of Providence* at an unspecified location along the Mississippi. The *City of Providence* was a side-wheel packet that was later converted to an excursion boat operating out of St. Louis. Built in 1880, it lasted until January 1910, when ice pushed it up against the bank. While efforts were being made to get the boat back in the water, it suddenly slipped in and sank for a total loss.

Well-dressed men, women, and children pose for a photo in the cavernous cabin of the *City of Providence*. The boat was originally owned by the Anchor Line, then sold to Columbia Excursion Company from St. Louis when Anchor went out of business. On June 15, 1888, tragedy struck about 30 miles above Memphis. A cylinder head on a port engine blew out, killing the striker engineer George Betts.

The stern-wheel packet *Josie Sivley,* the U.S. Engineering Department snagboat *Columbia,* and the stern-wheel towboat *Independence* line up along a Mississippi River landing. The *Sivley,* built in 1896, sank on the Sunflower River in Mississippi in 1900. The *Columbia* was built in 1877 as the *Colonel Hooker* and was purchased in 1888 by the U.S. Engineering Department. Renamed in 1894, it ran along the lower Mississippi through 1917, mostly out of Vicksburg.

The tenth and last steamboat carrying the name *Grey Eagle* is seen in the background along the Ohio River below Louisville. The men in the foreground are working on improvements to the Portland Canal, which diverted river traffic around the treacherous falls of the Ohio slightly downriver from Louisville. The canal opened in 1830 and was improved in stages over the years, the most recent of which was in the 1960s. It is still in use today.

A worker stands in front of the port engine on the *Cyclone,* a stern-wheel packet/rafter, in this photo from the 1890s. Built in 1891 in Stillwater, Minnesota, the *Cyclone* ran exclusively along the upper Mississippi between St. Paul and Wabasha, Minnesota. It burned on the ways at Wabasha on December 2, 1907.

The *Grey Eagle* docks at what appears to be a remote location along the Mississippi in this 1890s photo. Originally designed for the St. Louis to Peoria trade, the boat was too big to negotiate the turn (swing) bridges on the Illinois River. For the last eight years of its existence, the *Grey Eagle* ran excursions out of St. Louis in place of the *City of Providence*.

The packet side-wheeler *Dewey* is moored at dockside in New Orleans. Built in 1888 as the second *Kate Adams*, it was renamed in September 1898 after Admiral George Dewey, hero of the Battle of Manila Bay in the Spanish-American War fought that year. Under the ownership of the New Orleans–based Chalmette Packet Company, it ran from New Orleans as far north as Vicksburg and Memphis. It was sold in 1902 and renamed *Lotus Sims.*

In this 1898 photo, the stern-wheel rafter *Lafayette Lamb* ties up along the quay at Winona, Minnesota, near the overhead and swing span bridges across the upper Mississippi. Named for one of the boat owner's sons, the *Lafayette Lamb* was built in 1874 and lasted 30 years. After a succession of ownership changes, the boat was dismantled at Stillwater, its machinery going to the packet *Fountain City*.

THE NEW CENTURY AND THE
DECLINE OF STEAMBOATING

(1900–1919)

The first decade of the twentieth century started out well for the steamboats. Presidents Theodore Roosevelt in 1907 and William Howard Taft in 1909 boarded steamboats to visit cities along the Mississippi, accompanied by a flotilla of other steamboats in a patriotic display of pomp and panoply.

However, the steamboats' era of usefulness was slowly coming to an end. Railroads, which had been their rivals for passengers and freight since the mid-1800s, were finally gaining the upper hand. Advances in engineering technology enabled bridges to span the Mississippi and its many tributaries, allowing the rail companies to deliver their goods faster, more efficiently, and to more locales. As rail shipping prices dropped, steamboats lost their competitive advantage. And, to make matters worse, in those years of loosely regulated commerce, railroad bridges built over rivers were often too low for the steamboats to pass under.

Still, the steamboats hung in there for as long as they could. The romanticism that accompanied a steamboat journey continued to prevail. Many people still preferred the laid-back pace of a river journey over a noisy, unscenic, and often-dirty and uncomfortable train ride. The steam-powered towboats that performed their riverborne tasks continued to be indispensable. For example, in 1907 the giant stern-wheeler *Sprague* powered a tow of 60 coal barges covering 6.5 acres, a massive undertaking that would have required hundreds of rail cars at a much greater cost.

But even the towboats began to adapt to more modern, more practical technology and more fuel-efficient power sources. Coal began to replace wood as the primary fuel that powered a vessel's boilers. Later, propane would be used, then fuel oil, then diesel fuel. Screw-type propellers were beginning to replace paddle wheels.

Fewer steamboats were constructed during this period. Those built in earlier years continued to ply the waters of the Mississippi basin until they either wore out and were decommissioned, or they succumbed to one or more of the navigational hazards that had plagued their existence since the beginning. As steamboats, especially packets, went out of service, most of them were not replaced. One by one, once-prominent steamboat companies literally abandoned ship and went out of business. It was a sad time for fans of a storied method of transport.

The stern-wheel packet *America* plies the Mississippi. Built in 1898, this was the seventh of eight boats of the same name. It ran from New Orleans up the Ouachita River as far as Monroe, Louisiana, then later up to Vicksburg and Greenville. In 1924, a silent movie called *Magnolia* was filmed on board, and the boat was temporarily called the *Winfield Scott*. The *America* was laid up in New Orleans and foundered there on August 13, 1926.

The stern-wheeler *Belle of Calhoun* (left) and the side-wheeler *Belle of the Bends* tie up to the wharf in Vicksburg. The *Belle of Calhoun,* built in 1895, operated out of St. Louis. It sank twice, in 1914 and 1929, and was raised both times, only to burn beyond repair during the winter of 1930-31. The *Belle of the Bends,* built in 1898, also sank twice, in 1909 and 1910, before being converted to an excursion boat named *Liberty.*

A group of well-dressed women line the upper deck of the stern-wheel towboat *Eleonore,* which was converted into a packet after it burned at Memphis in September 1911. In June 1916, while running the Memphis-Ashport trade, it capsized 20 miles above Memphis, drowning several passengers and the ship's purser.

The stern-wheel packet *Georgia Lee* rests at dockside, probably somewhere along the Ohio River. Built in Jeffersonville in 1898, it made runs along the Ohio and Mississippi rivers between Memphis and Cincinnati. Named for the daughter of Captain James Lee (who also had a boat named for him), the *Georgia Lee* sank at Paducah in 1909 and was raised and restored. It was lost in ice at Memphis in January 1918, ironically alongside the *James Lee*.

The stern-wheel packet *City of Savannah* takes on freight at an unspecified location. Built in 1902, it was homeported at St. Louis and made runs along the Mississippi and Ohio rivers. In November 1909, it collided with a launch at Paducah and sank it, rescuing its two occupants. The *City of Savannah*'s officers were cleared by an investigation later that year. It sank two years later after hitting a snag in the Mississippi 22 miles above Cairo.

Two men move barrels on the dockside levee at St. Louis around 1903. In the background is an unidentifiable steamboat and the Eads Bridge that spans the river between St. Louis and East St. Louis, Illinois.

Crew members pose on the deck of the propane tugboat *General Abbot* in this photo from the early 1900s. Originally the *Maude H.*, the *General Abbot* was built in Baltimore in 1893 and bought there by the Mississippi River Commission in 1902. It was employed on the Mississippi River Fourth District by the Commission, then transferred to U.S. Corps of Engineers in New Orleans and renamed *Marengo*.

The *Belle of Calhoun* (left) and the *Corwin H. Spencer* leave the dock at St. Louis. The *Belle of Calhoun* was named for Miss Anna Wood, the "Belle of Calhoun County, Illinois," who won a contest run by the *Hardin (Illinois) Herald*. The *Spencer* was originally the *Hill City*, built in 1897. A side-wheeler, it ran excursions for visitors to the 1904 St. Louis World Exposition. A year later, it burned above Jefferson Barracks, Missouri.

Built in 1895 and originally named the *Virginia,* the *East St. Louis* seen in this photo got its name in 1916 after being purchased by the St. Louis and New Orleans Navigation Company. A year later, it was transformed into an excursion boat at Keokuk. Following a fire that destroyed the *Island Queen* and the *Morning Star* at Cincinnati in 1922, the *East St. Louis* was acquired by the destroyed ships' company and renamed *Island Belle.*

The pilothouse of the *Columbia* is seen from a pier after a 1903 excursion on the Ohio River. In September 1907, the stern-wheeler participated in the riverboat parade that carried President Theodore Roosevelt between Keokuk and Memphis. Under new owners from Peoria, the *Columbia* ran excursions on the Illinois River from 1912 until July 5, 1918, when it snagged in a fog and sank near Pekin, Illinois. Eighty-nine lives were lost.

Officers and crew of the stern-wheel packet *City of Saltillo* pose in this early 1900s photo. Built in 1904 and homeported in St. Louis, the boat hit a rock shore during a fog south of St. Louis on May 11, 1910, resulting in the loss of 12 lives, seven of whom were passengers. Edwin Pell, the ship's pilot at the time, lost his license, and Captain Harry Crane had his license suspended for six months.

In this early 1900s photo, three crew members look out from the upper deck of the stern-wheel towboat *Elinor* docked on the Mississippi. It was built in 1905 in Jeffersonville, Indiana, and received a new steel hull in 1924 at the Howard Ship Yard in Jeffersonville. This increased the boat's length by 21 feet. In 1930, it was completely rebuilt. Eleven years later, it was purchased by the Greenville Sand and Gravel Company of Greenville, Mississippi, and renamed the *W. W. Fischer*.

Spectators on shore watch as the stern-wheeler *Alda* steams up the White River near Clarendon, Arkansas, around 1905. Built in 1891 at Booneville, Missouri, the *Alda* was a low-draft packet specifically designed to run the shallower tributaries of the lower Mississippi, including the White, Sunflower, and Missouri rivers. Converted to freight and towboat status, it ran exclusively in the timber trade, making 49 trips from Clarendon to various logging camps during the 1909–1910 boating season.

Passengers aboard the side-wheel packet *David Swain* come ashore at Lacon, Illinois. Built and owned by the Swain family in 1906, it made Illinois River runs and was the last side-wheel packet on that river. It later began making Vicksburg to Natchez runs before being dismantled in Vidalia, Louisiana, in the early 1930s.

Cargo is unloaded from the *City of St. Joseph* in this early-twentieth-century photo. Built in 1901 as a stern-wheel packet in St. Joseph, Missouri, it made trips to the 1904 St. Louis World's Fair. In June 1911 while on a Memphis run, a flue collapsed, killing 18 deck crew members and injuring an engineer. Five years later, the boat was caught out high and dry at Luna Landing, Arkansas, remaining there until rescued and renamed the *Eclipse*.

A horse-drawn wagon awaits loading of cargo from the docked *City of St. Louis* side-wheel packet boat. The third of three boats bearing the name, the *City of St. Louis* was built in 1907 on the Mississippi as a harbor boat named *Erastus Wells*. The name was changed around 1932 when ownership changed hands. It ran until the mid-1940s and was finally dismantled when its usefulness waned.

The side-wheel harbor boat *Erastus Wells* is decked out in patriotic colors as it lies at anchor in Natchez, Mississippi. The occasion being celebrated is uncertain, but it is likely either one of two presidential journeys, Theodore Roosevelt in 1907 or William Howard Taft in 1909. Named after a former congressman from St. Louis, it was capable of holding 2,000 passengers at a time. After being sold in 1932, it was renamed *City of St. Louis*.

The *Grey Eagle* is decked out in patriotic bunting for a presidential visit, either Theodore Roosevelt in 1907 or Taft in 1909.

Following Spread: The Mississippi riverfront at Keokuk, Iowa, around 1907 shows rail yards and a bridge in the left background. Lying at the mouth of the Des Moines River, Keokuk was a key port along the Mississippi in the late nineteenth and early twentieth centuries.

The side-wheel packet *David Swain* waits ashore with horse-drawn carriages, probably along the Illinois River, where it ran in the early 1900s.

The rafter/excursion boat *Frontenac* takes on passengers at La Crosse while towing a barge behind it. A stern-wheeler built in 1896 at Wabasha, Minnesota, the *Frontenac* rafted for 11 years before it was remodeled into an excursion boat. It then operated out of St. Paul for about five years before being renamed *Prince* in 1912. Its engine came from the *Juniata*.

A crowd greets the stern-wheel packet/excursion boat *Columbia* at Red Wing, Minnesota. The eighth of eleven steamboats with the name, it was built in Stillwater, Minnesota, in 1900. In 1906, it was bought by a company in Florida and used during the construction of the FEC Railroad in the Florida Keys to Key West. It burned in the Panhandle at Milton, Florida, on March 13, 1911.

An engineer poses for this photograph in the engine room of the stern-wheel snagboat *Columbia.* An engineer's job on a steamboat was one of constant vigil, involving monitoring gauges, lubricating moving parts, and continually checking the boat's inner machinery to ensure smooth functioning. With fires and explosions a constant threat, there was little margin for error; a serious mishap resulting in extensive damage could cost an engineer his job, if not his life.

The writing on this photo indicates that on July 22 of an unspecified year, the *Columbia* is leaving New Boston, Illinois, on the upper Mississippi for an excursion to Aledo, Illinois. This is the same *Columbia* that participated in the riverborne procession for President Theodore Roosevelt from Keokuk to Memphis in 1907. It sank at Pekin, Illinois, in 1918 with the loss of 89 lives.

A close-up shows a group of passengers aboard the *Dubuque*. In July 1901, it sank at Keithsburg, Illinois, after ripping a 142-foot hole in its hull. It was later raised and restored. In November 1914, Captain Charles R. Martin, the boat's pilot, died at the wheel as the boat approached the Alton railroad bridge. The engineer on watch reacted quickly, calling on an off-watch pilot to right the boat's veering course.

Built in 1891 with a composite hull (iron framing with wooden planking), the stern-wheel towboat *Fury* belonged to the U.S. Corps of Engineers and operated in the upper Mississippi River's Rock Island and St. Paul districts. It was sold in 1931 to a private owner, who resold it eight years later. It towed a showboat in 1941 for Oscar Bloom of Chicago and was dismantled at Paducah in the fall of 1942, its parts sold for scrap.

In this 1909 photo, President Taft is seated at the end of this table of dignitaries aboard the harbor boat *Erastus Wells*. Built in 1907 at Grafton, Illinois, it operated out of St. Louis and was eventually remodeled as an excursion boat.

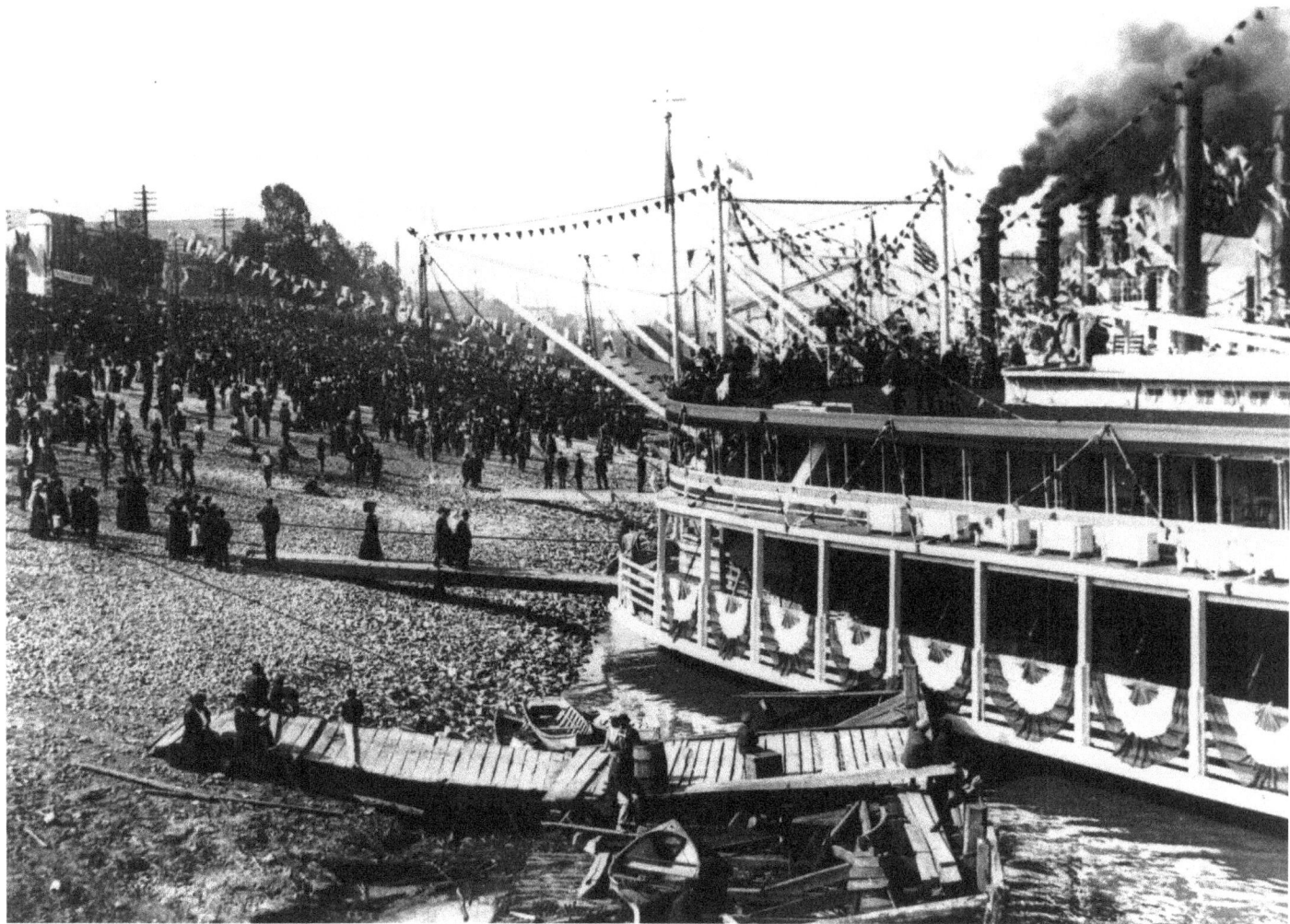

The *Grey Eagle* docks at Cape Girardeau, Missouri, in 1909. The bunting draped over the side of the boat and the banners streaming from the boat to the shore, along with the crowds on shore, all celebrate the visit of President Taft.

The stern-wheel towboat *Ada* churns along close to the shore of the Mississippi with a tow in this early-twentieth-century photo. It was built in 1889 at Keokuk as a single-stack, small-job towboat in service for the U.S. Engineering Department, Rock Island District. Assigned to U.S. Engineering in St. Paul in 1922, it was off the lists by June 30, 1923. It became a U.S. lighthouse tender and wintered at Fountain City, Wisconsin.

Spectators on the shore watch two stern-wheel towboats out of Pittsburgh run side by side under a suspension bridge across the Ohio River. The *Gleaner,* built in 1896, sank in a storm on June 13, 1912, at Plaquemine, Louisiana, along with 20 barges of coal. The *Boaz* in this picture is the third of four that bore the name. It lasted from 1882 to 1925 before being mothballed and eventually dismantled on the Monongahela River.

Pilot George N. Ashby grips the steering wheel in the pilothouse of the stern-wheel packet *Ed Myer*. Built in Jeffersonville, it ran along the Ohio, Cumberland, Missouri, and Mississippi rivers. Because of its low-draft hull design, it was often chartered out during low water between Louisville and Evansville. It was lost in ice at Helena, Arkansas, on January 23, 1918.

Three crew members stand on the dock in front of the stern-wheel towboat *Ada*.

Deckhands work to secure the mooring lines of the *Dubuque* to the dock at an unspecified location along the Mississippi River.

A small group of passengers awaits the arrival of the *Dubuque* at Dallas City, Illinois, in this early 1900s photo. In the background, the high water level is visible against the trees on shore.

The stern-wheel packet/excursion boat *East St. Louis* sits tethered to the shore of an unspecified town during a flood. The automobile seen in the front of the picture represents a harbinger of future transportation. By the middle of the twentieth century, much of the freight formerly carried by steamboats would be transported by trains and trucks.

An early-twentieth-century auto is driven inside the stern-wheel towboat *Ellen*. The boat was built in 1907 and named for the wife of W. W. Cargill, founder of the multinational agribusiness firm, who used it as a rafter and pleasure cruiser. It was retrofitted with a steel hull around 1930, and air conditioning and an elevator were installed for a visit by President Franklin D. Roosevelt that was canceled. The *Ellen* sank in 1918, was raised, and lasted until 1944.

The *Mary H. Miller* sits on a floating drydock in Vicksburg while having work done on its underside. Boats in some drydocks could be lifted so that workmen could get under the hull, check for damage, and do repairs if necessary. The *Mary H. Miller*, a stern-wheel packet built in 1904, operated on the Yazoo River, which empties into the Mississippi at Vicksburg. It sank and was lost above Yazoo City in 1910.

A crowd of bystanders watches the flight of an early biplane as the stern-wheel packet *Alabama* sits moored in the background. Built in 1912, *Alabama* was the last of six Mississippi steamboats to bear the name. It ran along the Ohio and Tennessee rivers carrying passengers and freight, and it ran as far south on the Mississippi as Memphis. In 1934, it was rebuilt as a quarter boat.

Passengers embark and disembark from the *Columbia* at St. Louis on August 16, 1916. A bridge under construction is seen in the background.

The *Grey Eagle* passes under the Eads Bridge at St. Louis in this early-twentieth-century photo. A handful of pedestrians watch from the bridge above.

In this photo taken by Alene Stottlebower between 1915 and 1919, the *East St. Louis* is lit up at night on the Mississippi. In the years just prior to passage of the Women's Suffrage Amendment, the boat's parent company—the Streckfus Line—hired one of the few female pilots on the river, Mary Hulett.

The stern-wheeler *Golden Fleece* lies docked at an undocumented location along the Ohio River in this photo taken between 1913 and 1919. As a packet, it ran between Paducah, Kentucky, and Golconda, Illinois. In 1925, it was sold to a buyer who converted it into a towboat at Mound City, Illinois. As a towboat it was renamed *Julia O'Sullivan* and later *Frank Woods*.

A crowd gathers on the Memphis shore to watch the *Georgia Lee* slowly sink into the Mississippi after being crushed by ice in January 1918. Workers using skiffs to reach the foundering boat try to salvage what they can before it goes completely under.

A distinguished-looking unidentified man stands next to the ornate harbor bell on the deck of the *Erastus Wells*.

An unidentified man and woman prepare to lift off in a hot air balloon from the bow of the *Erastus Wells* as crew officers and unidentified dignitaries look on. In the early twentieth century, hot air ballooning was a popular pastime for those who could afford it. Boat decks were often used as launch sites because of favorable wind currents over a wide body of water.

The hot air balloon lifts off from the bow of the *Erastus Wells* as spectators from the dock cheer its passengers on.

THE FINAL YEARS: END OF THE PACKET ERA

(1920–1939)

The first half of the period between the two world wars was a time of record prosperity in America. The second half was a period of record job loss, unemployment, and incalculable misery. Going from the glamour and glitz of the Roaring Twenties to the sullen and somber Great Depression was a massive step downward for large numbers of Americans.

Steamboats and steamboat companies were not spared the fate the average citizen was encountering. Ridership on the few remaining packet ships declined, tonnage carried or towed by the workboats declined, and of course, steamboat company revenues declined in direct proportion to the losses in ridership and cargo transport.

Nonetheless, a handful of storied packet vessels and their parent companies managed to literally stay afloat, and even a few that survive today were constructed during this time period—most notably the *Delta Queen* and the *Belle of Louisville.* The *Capitol,* the *America,* the *Gordon C. Greene,* and others continued to ply the Mississippi, as steamboats had done for more than a century, offering their passengers all the amenities their needs and lifestyles required. The Eagle Packet Company, with a generational history dating back to the early 1860s, hung in with its last survivor, the *Golden Eagle,* until the mid-1940s.

Heartwarming river stories abounded during this time. One of America's first female riverboat captains, Mary Becker "Ma" Greene, wife of Captain Gordon C. Greene, gave birth to the couple's son Tom aboard the *Greenland* at Point Pleasant, West Virginia, while icebound in February 1904. (A year earlier she had beaten her husband in a steamboat race between Pittsburgh and Cincinnati.) In the 1920s, Tom Greene became a river pilot himself with a boat named after him, and, in tandem with "Captain Ma" (also nicknamed "Old Ma'am River"), they steered boats of their family's fleet up and down the rivers until well into the 1940s. Captain Tom, unwilling to be without his wife and children, often brought them along for the ride, making riverboating a true family affair for three generations.

The stern-wheeler *Capitol* steams north on the Mississippi toward the railroad bridge in the distance connecting La Crosse, Wisconsin, and Minnesota. Converted from the *Dubuque* to an excursion vessel by Streckfus Steamers in 1920, it ran out of St. Louis and also operated in New Orleans for a time. On May 5, 1923, it carried dignitaries at the opening of the Industrial Canal, which connected the Mississippi with Lake Pontchartrain in New Orleans.

Carrying freight for the *Helen Blair* stern-wheeler, horse-drawn wagons head for the dock through the streets of this unidentifiable yet sizable town (possibly the boat's home port of Burlington, Iowa). Built in 1896 as the *Urania,* the *Helen Blair* was renamed by a new owner in 1901 after his daughter. In 1910, it sank in seven feet of water after hitting an obstruction in the channel below Davenport. Raised and repaired, it continued to operate until 1919 and was dismantled the following year.

The *Capitol* is docked at Alton, Illinois, in this 1920 photo. Converted into an excursion boat from the *Dubuque,* it ran until the summer of 1945, when it was dismantled at St. Louis.

This shot, with a view of the dining room below, was taken inside the side-wheel packet *Cincinnati* from the upper level of the two-story main cabin. The sixth and final steamboat bearing the name, this *Cincinnati* put on a lot of mileage during its brief eight-year lifespan, running the Ohio and Mississippi rivers between Pittsburgh, Cincinnati, Louisville, and New Orleans and points in between.

In this postcard view recorded on June 18, 1920, the Streckfus Steamers excursion boat *Capitol* prepares to come ashore to a large crowd waiting at Bellevue, Iowa.

A large crowd gathers along the riverfront to greet the *Capitol* in this unspecified location on Labor Day 1922. One of the most elegant steamboats in its class, the *Capitol* measured 257 by 51 feet and was powered by four boilers with a capacity of 250 pounds per square inch. Its paddle wheel was 25 feet in diameter with 30-foot buckets.

Roustabouts work on the deck of the stern-wheel packet/excursion boat *Golden Eagle* in this 1920s photo. Originally the cotton packet *William Garig,* it was sold to the Eagle Packet Company of St. Louis in 1918 and renamed. It ran between St. Louis and Peoria, then between St. Louis and Cape Girardeau. Sold to a Cincinnati company in 1935, it made tourist runs to St. Paul, Chattanooga, Cincinnati, and Nashville.

Passengers aboard the stern-wheel packet *Alabama* look out from the deck in this 1923 photo. Built at Point Pleasant, West Virginia, in 1912, the *Alabama* was the last regular steam packet on the Tennessee River before it began to be dammed in the late 1920s. It ran regularly between Cincinnati and Louisville, then was chartered in 1932 for a company in Memphis, where it was retired and turned into a quarter boat.

Following Spread: The stern-wheeler *Cape Girardeau* lies docked among other boats on the St. Louis riverfront downriver from the Eads Bridge. The third of three packets bearing the name, the *Cape Girardeau* was built in 1923 for the Louisville to St. Louis trade, and later to New Orleans. In 1935, it was sold to the Greene family and rechristened *Gordon C. Greene* in memory of the captain who died in 1927. His widow Mary and son Tom were co-captains.

Deckhands (from left to right) J. Ellis, unidentified man, Gene Masters, and Robert Bradford pose aboard the stern-wheel excursion boat *Belle of Louisville* in this 1925 photo. Built in 1914, it was formerly the *Idlewild* and the *Avalon* and was given its most recent name in 1962. For many years starting in 1963, the *Belle of Louisville* raced the *Delta Queen* at Louisville during the annual Kentucky Derby. It is still in service today.

In 1925, a crowd gathers on shore and on the deck of the *Cincinnati* (right) for the dedication of Dam 36 on the Ohio River. On May 24, 1928, between Carrollton and Madison, the boat collided with the *Belfont,* and engineer Homer Johnston was killed. Sold to Streckfus Steamers in 1932, the boat was torn down to its hull and rebuilt as the excursion boat *President.*

The stern-wheel packet *America* lies wrecked along the shore near Baton Rouge, Louisiana, on August 13, 1926. Before the boat sank, its roof bell was salvaged and later mounted over the grave of Captain LeVerrier Cooley, a former owner and captain of the boat, who died on December 19, 1931, and was buried in New Orleans.

The stern-wheel towboat *Aldebaran* moves a dredge in shallow water along the upper Mississippi. Built in 1924 at Wabasha, Minnesota, it was sold the following year to the U.S. Department of Engineering and used as a survey boat on the lower Mississippi River. Captain Rush Burnside and others bought the boat at Memphis in December 1934 and renamed it *Rush Krodell*.

The *A. W. Armstrong* pushes a tow along the Mississippi in this late 1920s photo. Built in 1925 at Mound City, Illinois, the *A. W. Armstrong* was a stern-wheel towboat used to tow large construction equipment, including engines, down the Mississippi River. Much of the equipment from the towboat *Transit* was used in its construction. It "turned turtle" (flipped over) in a windstorm near St. Genevieve, Missouri, on June 25, 1930.

Festooned in flags and bunting, the stern-wheel towboat *Exporter* takes part in a boat parade for President Herbert Hoover at Dam 53 on the Ohio River. Built in 1895, the *Exporter* ran for 14.5 hours from St. Louis to Cairo to bring the *Henry Lourey* in tow after it broke down the following year. It was sold in April 1901 and went to Pittsburgh, where it towed coal south until sold again in 1918. It was dismantled in 1936.

The side-wheel packet *America* lies docked outside a sizable city, possibly Cincinnati or Louisville, in this photo taken around 1930. Built in 1917, the *America* ran the Ohio River between these two cities. In 1928, it raced the *Cincinnati* at Louisville and could have won but was prevented by management from doing so for reasons now unknown. On September 8, 1930, while laid up for the winter above Jeffersonville, Indiana, it burned. Arson was suspected but never proven.

In this spectacular panorama, the *Golden Eagle* prepares to come ashore at an unidentified town on the upper Mississippi. The workboat *Sea Lion* is at lower-right. On June 14, 1941, the *Golden Eagle* hit a submerged dike and sank, but it was raised and repaired when the river level fell. However, in the early morning hours of May 17, 1947, the boat sank off Tower Island. It was the last wood-hulled stern-wheel packet on the Mississippi.

Like a scene out of a Mark Twain novel, two young boys on shore at Clinton, Iowa, watch the paddle wheel of the *Golden Eagle* churn down the Mississippi. After completion of the locks and dams on the upper Mississippi, the *Golden Eagle* was the first packet boat in many years to put in at St. Paul. A gold-colored ball swung between its twin smokestacks to identify the boat.

The *Golden Eagle* is docked along the levee at an unspecified location. After the boat sank in 1947, a Golden Eagle Club was formed in St. Louis to commemorate the vessel. The *Golden Eagle*'s salvaged pilothouse is in the Missouri Historical Society's exhibits at Jefferson National Expansion Memorial in St. Louis.

Boathands aboard the side-wheel snagboat *Horatio G. Wright* work to remove a snag from the Mississippi. Huge trees, like the one in the background, presented one of the deadliest navigational hazards faced by riverboats on the Mississippi and its tributaries. Thick, jagged branches lurking just below the water's surface could tear a hole in a wooden hull and did so many times. The *Horatio G. Wright,* built in 1880, lasted until 1941, when it was dismantled.

A set of railroad train wheels pulled from the Mississippi at St. Charles, Missouri, sit on the deck of the *Horatio G. Wright* in this 1931 photo. With its steel hull, the boat was not as vulnerable to snags as the earlier wood-hulled models, and its overall construction allowed it to do heavy lifting work. An excellent model of the boat, which was dismantled in 1941, is displayed at the Museum of Science and Industry in Chicago.

Roustabouts enjoy a moment of relaxation on the bow of the *City of St. Louis* in this 1933 photo. This was the third and final boat bearing the name; it was the former *Erastus Wells* built in 1907. The name was changed when the boat was sold in 1932. It was later resold to a dredging company, then to Allied Oil Company in February 1944 before being dismantled.

The *General Allen* towboat ashore on the upper Mississippi. Seen in the photo are William Henning (master in the pilothouse), Allen Fiedler and H. N. Auderly of St. Paul District Engineers Office (on top deck), Andrew Gevreralm, Robert Grossell, Alfred Mehringer (main deck hands), Ben Harvey (engine room), and R. N. Smith (lower deck). Four visitors watch the boat from the shore. Built in 1915 at Jeffersonville, it was originally the *Minnesota,* a pleasure boat for doctors William and Charles Mayo, founders of the Mayo Clinic. Sold to the St. Paul District U.S. Engineers in 1922, it was renamed *General Allen.* The Central Barge Company bought the *General Allen* from USE in 1943 and reverted it to the original name *Minnesota.*

The stern-wheel towboat *Ellen* passes the swing bridge as it steams through Mississippi River Lock and Dam Number 15 between Rock Island and Davenport on March 23, 1932. It was the first steamboat to pass through the main lock heading upstream.

The stern-wheel packet/excursion liner *Gordon C. Greene* passes under the suspension bridge between Prairie du Chien, Wisconsin, and Marquette, Iowa. Built in 1923 as the *Cape Girardeau,* it was renamed by the Greene family, who bought the boat from Eagle Packet Company in 1935. Operating the boat was a family affair, with Captain Mary Becker "Ma" Greene relieving son Tom at the wheel. Unwilling to leave his wife and children behind, Captain Tom often brought them with him.

Deckhands lower the gangplank of the *Capitol* as the boat approaches its landing in La Crosse around 1935.

The *Golden Eagle* is seen from a riverside park in Fort Madison, Iowa, in 1935. On April 22, 1939, during the World's Fair in San Francisco, the *Golden Eagle* took part in an unusual publicity stunt: a mock race with the *Delta Queen* on the Sacramento River. On the Mississippi, the *Golden Eagle* made its run more quickly than the *Delta Queen* did for the same distance on the Sacramento.

Laborers working to strengthen the levee along the Mississippi take a break, with the stern-wheel towboat *Daniel Boone* in the background. Logs brought in by the towboat are used as riprap, solid building materials laid in place to slow down levee erosion. Built in 1925, the *Daniel Boone* was purchased by Phillips Petroleum for its hull. It was then used as a landing barge at their tank farm below East St. Louis before being dismantled in 1943.

In this 1930s photo, passengers disembark from the *Golden Eagle* and ascend a steep incline in an unspecified location.

The *General Allen* passes along one of the most scenic stretches of the upper Mississippi in Minnesota as it tows a barge. In August 1939, it went up the Minnesota River for about 30 miles to Shakopee with a quarter boat, derrick, and three barges, making a rare visit to that small river port. During that trip, the boat's tow had to be broken to navigate around "the bends," but it survived intact.

The *Alexander Mackenzie* steams up the Mississippi past Riverside Park in La Crosse. A stern-wheel towboat that ran up the Illinois and Mississippi rivers between 1939 and 1954, it had powerful engines and a steel hull. In April 1946, an engine room accident killed engineer Robert Brown. The boat was transferred to Mississippi Valley Barge Line Company and brought to Cincinnati in 1952, then sold to another barge company and dismantled at Port Amherst, West Virginia.

In this late 1930s photo, the *Golden Eagle* is docked at Hannibal, Missouri, Mark Twain's boyhood home. In the background is the Mark Twain Memorial Lighthouse on Cardiff Hill, built in 1935 for the centennial of Twain's birth. It never served as a navigational aid but rather as a permanent memorial to the Steamboat Era's most prolific author.

A pilot guides the stern-wheel inspection towboat *Gen. John Newton* as other crew members in the pilothouse look on. With its steel-hull construction, the *Newton* enjoyed an incredibly long lifespan for a steamboat—58 years (1899–1957). Owned by the Mississippi River Commission, it was a coal burner for 40 years before converting to oil. It was declared surplus in 1957, sold to the University of Minnesota, and converted into the *Minnesota Centennial Showboat*.

Passengers dine on the starboard guard of the *Golden Eagle* on a trip from St. Louis to St. Paul between June 20 and 30, 1939.

PLEASURE CRUISING: THE RISING POPULARITY OF STEAMBOAT EXCURSIONS

(1940–1999)

As traditional packet boats disappeared from the Mississippi River waterscape, a new era in pleasure boating dawned. The mystique of the river and its port cities, both large and small, continued to be a magnet for tourists and sightseers from this country and many others. No longer jamming up their decks with bulky cotton bales and other large freight, most of the steamboats that survived the transition found new life as excursion boats or "day liners."

The Greene family from Cincinnati took a major step in this direction with their 1946 purchase of the *Delta Queen* from its previous owners on California's Sacramento River. Floated through the Panama Canal and powered up the Mississippi and Ohio rivers, it was turned into an excursion vessel that frequently raced other boats on the two rivers. The by-now-legendary Captain Mary "Ma" Greene ruled the roost aboard the *Delta Queen,* playing the gregarious hostess, and even dancing a Virginia reel in the boat's cabin two days before her death at age 80. Eventually the boat ended up in New Orleans, where it ran lengthy excursions as far as St. Louis, Cincinnati, and Pittsburgh until it was decommissioned in 2008.

Other still-surviving former packet boats joined in the competition for the tourist dollar and converted to excursion vessels. The vintage 1915 *Idlewild* became the *Avalon* in 1948 and the *Belle of Louisville* (which survives today) in 1962. Newer, sleeker, and larger craft like the *Admiral,* homeported in St. Louis, joined the fleet of Mississippi River pleasure craft. With an ultra-modern look and even more modern amenities—including fully air-conditioned staterooms—the *Admiral* enjoyed a 30-year run before being permanently moored in the shadow of the Gateway Arch.

By the closing years of the twentieth century and into the early years of the twenty-first, excursion steamboats had become major tourist attractions for their host cities; objects of curiosity, awe, and inspiration. Newer boats built on models of their predecessors began to reclaim the waterways, offering steamboat aficionados unique glimpses into a storied past, along with fun and sumptuous amenities. The best of the old and the best of the new: today's still-operating riverboats have them both.

The stern-wheeler *Capitol* steams along the Mississippi near La Crosse in this 1940 photo.

Passengers disembark from the *Capitol* in St. Paul on September 9, 1940.

Cars park on the levee while the *Capitol* is tied up along the Mississippi in this photo taken on September 28, 1941. In remote locations where there were no adequate docking facilities, steamboats simply dropped anchor as close to the shore as they could, then ran a crude wooden gangplank to the river bank. The boats' shallow-draft hulls enabled them to stay afloat in just a few feet of water.

Construction on the side-wheel excursion boat *Admiral* is seen from the boat's roof at St. Louis with the Eads Bridge in the background. Built in 1940 from the hull of the former railroad transfer boat *Albatross,* the *Admiral* became the largest passenger vessel on U.S. inland waterways. It was 374 feet long and 92 feet wide and was the first all-steel inland steamer. It had five decks, full air conditioning, and was capable of carrying 4,400 to 5,000 passengers.

The *Capitol* is docked near the suspension bridge at Prairie du Chien, Wisconsin, in this 1941 photo.

Repairs are made to the stern-wheel packet/excursion boat *Delta Queen* at the Todd Johnson Shipyard in New Orleans. From the 1970s until 2008, the *Delta Queen* ran excursions from a few days to a few weeks out of its home port of New Orleans, going as far upriver as St. Louis, Cincinnati, and Pittsburgh. Built in 1926, it made its final journey in 2009 to Chattanooga, Tennessee, where it was converted into a stationary luxury hotel.

A sailor stands aboard the stern-wheel towboat *General Ashburn*. Built in 1927, the boat was named for Major General Thomas Q. Ashburn. Owned by the Federal Barge Line and designed by T. Reese Tarn, this boat, along with the *Wynoka*, took part in the opening of the Peoria terminal in June 1931. It also served in the St. Louis–Kansas City trade in the fall of 1935. It was purchased by Hatfield Campbell Creek Coal Company and renamed *J. T. Hatfield* in 1945.

Dancer Mary Trabert of Milwaukee, Wisconsin, entertains passengers aboard the *Gordon C. Greene* on March 23, 1942. Originally built as a coal burner, it was converted into an oil burner in 1941. Captain Tom Greene let many youngsters ride for free to gain the experience of working aboard an excursion vessel. Co-captain Mary B. Greene was a well-loved hostess, with nearly 60 years of active piloting. She died at 80 in the cabin of the *Delta Queen* in 1949.

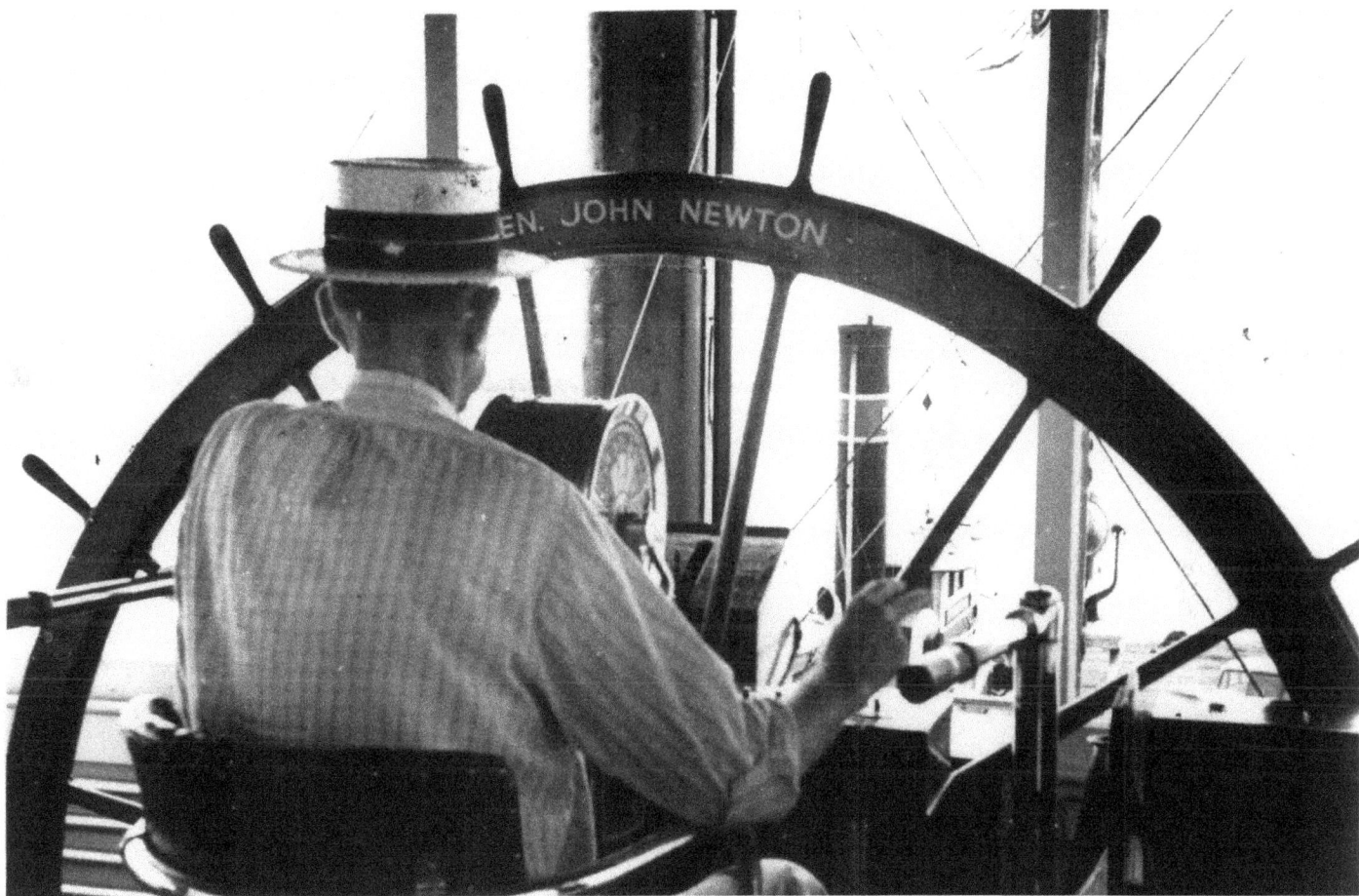

This view from the pilothouse of the *General John Newton* faces forward, with the pilot at the wheel. It measured 150 feet long, 28 feet at its widest point, and 7.5 feet in hull depth. The boat's first captain, Joe Pierce, ran the boat for 37 years until he retired at age 70 in 1936, the same year sponsons were added to the boat's hull.

In this photo taken around 1943, the stern-wheel packet/excursion boat *Idlewild* discharges passengers as it idles ashore at La Crosse. Built in 1914, it made its first run from Pittsburgh to Memphis early the following year. Before being sold in 1947 and renamed the *Avalon* a year later, the *Idlewild* ran the Mississippi, Ohio, Tennessee, Cumberland, Illinois, and Missouri rivers. It also operated at one time as a ferryboat.

A woman passenger disembarks from the *Admiral* at St. Louis with the Eads Bridge at left. Initially owned by Streckfus Steamers, the boat was converted to diesel-powered propellers—one in each paddlebox—over the winter of 1973-74. Its streamlined, enclosed, Art Deco appearance stood out in contrast to earlier steamboats that had open-air decks. For many years it was a familiar sight, cruising the Mississippi upriver and downriver from St. Louis.

Passengers sit at umbrella-sheltered tables on the lido deck of the *Admiral* during a cruise from St. Louis. The *Admiral* cruised the Mississippi for 39 years before being permanently moored near the Eads Bridge in 1979. During a $30 million renovation by the SS Admiral Partners, the engines were removed, and much of the interior was stripped of its Art Deco trim and fittings before the boat was converted into a floating casino.

Two young girls on shore at Marquette, Iowa, wave to the *Gordon C. Greene* near the bridge to Wisconsin in this 1944 photo. After its days as an excursion steamer ended in 1952, the *Greene* became a hotel in Portsmouth, Ohio, then a restaurant in Owensboro, Kentucky, then went to Bradenton, Florida, where a tourist attraction venture failed. It ended up in St. Louis in 1964 as a successful restaurant near the Eads Bridge, but three years later it burned and sank.

A group of white-shirted young men stand on a hillside watching the *Golden Eagle* pass on the river below. The river is not identified but, because of its narrow width and the height of the mountains in the background, it can be presumed to be either the Cumberland or the Tennessee. The *Golden Eagle* was known to have made runs on those rivers into the interiors of Kentucky and Tennessee.

The stern-wheel towboat *Alexander Mackenzie* pushes an 11-barge tow, plus a fuel barge, through the draw of the Milwaukee Road pontoon railroad bridge between Marquette, Iowa, and Prairie du Chien, Wisconsin. The suspension bridge between the two states is in the background.

The *Golden Eagle* cruises past two men fishing from a riverside park along the Mississippi in this photo taken in June 1946. Less than a year later, the boat would become history, running aground and sinking at Grand Tower Island, Illinois, on May 17, 1947.

The long, colorful history of the *Golden Eagle* awaits a lonely, watery grave as it slowly sinks after running aground at Grand Tower Island, Illinois, in May 1947. Workers try to salvage what they can before the boat goes under. With its demise, the glorious era of the wood-hulled stern-wheel packets on the Mississippi River came to an end.

A grim-faced purser, Bill Hess is seen on Grand Tower Island in the early morning daylight of May 17, 1947, with the grounded wreckage of the *Golden Eagle* in the background. The mishap occurred around 1:30 that morning, and all passengers were safely evacuated. It was the first and last run the boat made under its final owner, Herman T. Pott of St. Louis Shipbuilding and Steel Company, who had bought it only two months earlier.

Several of these well-dressed matronly ladies seem unusually cheerful despite being temporarily inconvenienced and stranded on Grand Tower Island after the *Golden Eagle* ran aground. Sitting on salvaged chairs, surrounded by their salvaged luggage, and awaiting rescue are (left to right) Mrs. Harrington, Mrs. Elsie Fischer of Milwaukee, Mrs. Crawford, and Miss Pfeiffer. An unknown photographer aboard the boat took a series of pictures of the boat's last voyage, which ended here on May 17, 1947.

A smartly uniformed, aging captain—possibly Ben Winters—is seen in the pilothouse at the wheel of the *Idlewild* in this classic river lore photo taken in August 1947. With its steel hull and solid construction, the *Idlewild* and its successors *Avalon* and the *Belle of Louisville* have enjoyed a long lifespan, from 1914 to the present. The *Idlewild* measured 157.5 feet long and 36 feet wide, with a five-foot hull depth. It ran on three boilers.

The stern-wheel excursion boat *Avalon* is moored at dockside in La Crosse. Built in 1915 as the *Idlewild,* the *Avalon* was given its new name in 1948 to grant the deathbed wish of Captain Ben Winters, who had worked aboard the first *Avalon,* which ran between 1898 and 1906 primarily along the Ohio River and its tributaries. While entering the Emsworth Lock on the Ohio on May 24, 1958, the boat's engine failed, and it hit the lower gate, injuring 23 people. It last saw service in 1982.

A woman sells postcards, souvenirs, and sundries aboard the *Delta Queen* in this 1948 photo. Possibly the most widely traveled steamboat ever, its steel framework was fabricated in Glasgow, Scotland, then shipped to San Francisco and assembled in the 1920s for service to Sacramento along the Sacramento River. Ornate, with modern conveniences and comforts—including air conditioning in the most expensive staterooms—it ran there until the early 1940s, when a highway between the two cities took its place.

The *Avalon* prepares to dock at McGregor, Iowa, in this 1949 photograph. Seen on deck are Captain Ernest E. Wagner (standing on the hull to the right of the steam exhaust vent), Captain Edgar Mayberry (on the portside landing), and other crew and passengers. In 1961, after taking a boatload of Girl Scouts from Memphis to New Orleans and returning another group to Memphis, Captain Wagner and his first mate Clarke Hawley were invested as official Girl Scouts.

Cars park on the levee at St. Louis near the *Admiral* in this 1950s photo.

The *Avalon* lies moored at a busy port, possibly Louisville or Cincinnati, in this 1950 photo. In 1962, the boat was sold at auction to a judge from Jefferson County Fiscal Court in Louisville and renamed the *Belle of Louisville*.

In this sweeping panorama taken from the bluffs above McGregor, Iowa, the *Avalon* loads passengers at the landing while the *Gordon C. Greene* (seen at midstream) glides in for a landing. The *Greene* did not make regularly scheduled stops at McGregor, but it would do so if notified ahead of time that passengers wished to be picked up there.

Passengers sit and stand around the massive dance floor of the *Avalon* before the live entertainment gets started.

The *Avalon* is moored ashore at Rock Island, Illinois, in 1953. Davenport, Iowa, directly across the Mississippi, is in the background.

Gona, a propeller towboat built in 1944, steams past an unidentified small river town. Operating under the auspices of the Inland Waterways Corporation during World War II, the boat went through a rapid succession of owners both before and after the war. In 1948, the boat's whistle was composed of whistles from the dredges *McGregor* and *Fort Gage*. The roof bell came from the ferry *Julius Walsh*. *Gona* was decommissioned in 1965.

The *Delta Queen* passes through the open swing span of the Milwaukee Railroad pontoon bridge at Marquette, Iowa, in 1956. During World War II, it was used as a yard ferryboat in San Francisco Bay. Later it ran excursions from New Orleans and was declared a National Historic Landmark. It was also given a presidential exemption from the law against overnight cruise ships with wooden superstructures. That exemption allowed it to operate until the late 2000s.

The *Delta Queen* rests at dockside. During its long, colorful history, the boat logged hundreds of thousands of miles between Scotland, San Francisco, New Orleans, and other points in the Mississippi River watershed. It revived the tradition of steamboat racing against other paddle wheelers, especially the *Belle of Louisville* during the Kentucky Derby and the *Natchez* in New Orleans. During its heyday in New Orleans, it was in a fleet that included the larger and newer *Mississippi Queen* and *American Queen*.

The *Avalon* crew poses for this shot while docked at St. Paul on August 22, 1958. Included are everyone from the captain (master) to the watchmen, deckhands, engineers, strikers, firemen, cabin boys, cooks, maids, and even the bandleader and musicians. African-Americans were still being relegated to the entertainment and the more menial jobs onboard, but with the Steamboat Era coming to an end, other opportunities began opening up for them in more technologically oriented transportation jobs.

The *Avalon* is lit up at night while docked in La Crosse on August 22, 1958.

This auction bill in the May 12, 1962, issue of the *Waterways Journal* advertises the bankruptcy sale of the *Avalon* while it was tied up in Cincinnati. In small print, the ad lists the boat's dimensions and amenities and possible uses of the boat for the buyer. The sale took place May 24, and the high bidder was Jefferson County court judge Marlow Cook. The boat was restored and renamed the *Belle of Louisville*.

187

The *Belle of Louisville* crew dines below deck in this photo from around 1964. From left to right are striker Chester LaHue, carpenter Bill Ellis, chief engineer David Crecelious, assistant engineer Arthur Rees (standing), and Captain Paul Underwood. The *Belle of Louisville* was built in 1914 as the *Idlewild*, then became the *Avalon* before taking on its present name. It still operates today as an excursion boat and races other steamboats during the Kentucky Derby.

The *Cap'n Howder*, a screw propeller towboat, is seen upbound at mile 32 on the upper Mississippi in this October 10, 1965, photo. Built in 1950 to honor veteran riverboat captain John L. Howder, it represented an advance in riverboat technology. Screw propellers with blades that cut smoothly through the water were smaller and easier to service than bulky paddle wheels.

Following Spread: The *Admiral* is docked at the St. Louis riverfront at night. An August 19, 2008, *Post-Dispatch* story reported that Pinnacle Entertainment, the current owner, had considered moving the boat north around the Chain of Rocks and wants to retain the casino's license. However, without a major overhaul, the vessel may not pass the required Coast Guard inspection in 2010, in which case it would end up being scrapped.

The *Admiral* lies moored at dockside in St. Louis with the Gateway Arch soaring in the background. Completed in 1965, the Arch is 630 feet high and commemorates President Thomas Jefferson and the nation's westward expansion in the 1800s. Trams running to the top of the Arch carry visitors up for spectacular views of the Mississippi River and the city. Exhibits at the foot of the Arch display artifacts and old photos and prints of the St. Louis riverfront in the nineteenth and early twentieth centuries, some of which show steamboats that were operating at the time.

The stern-wheel excursion boat, *Belle of Cincinnati,* is decked out in patriotic regalia for the Fourth of July while docked in New Orleans in 1999. The boat's owner, Captain Alan Bernstein, is in the dark shirt leaning over the bunting that hangs from the middle deck. The boat was in New Orleans for repairs and to tow the Millennium World Peace Bell to its permanent home in Newport, Kentucky, across the Ohio River from Cincinnati.

The Millennium Peace Bell is seen on a barge being towed behind the *Belle of Cincinnati* in this photo taken on July 4, 1999. The excursion paddle wheeler *Natchez,* built in 1975 as the twelfth boat bearing that name, is docked in the background along the New Orleans riverfront.

Notes on the Photographs

These notes, listed by page number, attempt to include all aspects known of the photographs. Each of the photographs is identified by the page number, photograph's title or description, photographer and collection, archive, and call or box number when applicable. Although every attempt was made to collect available data, in some cases complete data was unavailable due to the age and condition of some of the photographs and records.

II THEODORE ROOSEVELT ON THE MISSISSIPPI
Library of Congress
LC-USZ62-123512

VI COLONEL T. H. JUDSON, LECOMPTE, AND MILTON RELF
University of Wisconsin-La Crosse
Col. T. H. Judson 38393

X GUNBOAT SIGNAL
Library of Congress
LC-USZ62-62499

3 ALECK SCOTT
University of Wisconsin-La Crosse
Aleck Scott 6730

4 FEDERAL ARCH
University of Wisconsin-La Crosse
Federal Arch 29310

5 GOLDEN ERA
University of Wisconsin-La Crosse
Golden Era 33252

6 DES MOINES
University of Wisconsin-La Crosse
Des Moines 7688

7 DR. KANE
University of Wisconsin-La Crosse
Dr. Kane 34853

8 GUNBOAT BROWN
Library of Congress
LC-USZ62-62362

9 FORT HINDMAN
Library of Congress
LC-USZ62-113172

10 TENNESSEE
Library of Congress
LC-USZ62-62369

11 BOAT AT NATCHEZ
Library of Congress
LC-USZ62-62365

12 SULTANA
Library of Congress
LC-USZ62-48778

13 GREY EAGLE, EIGHTH OF TEN
University of Wisconsin-La Crosse
Grey Eagle(B) 28648

14 DEER LODGE
University of Wisconsin-La Crosse
Deer Lodge 36623

15 COLORADO AND DENVER
University of Wisconsin-La Crosse
Colorado 11026

16 CORNELIA, HENRY AMES, AND LIZZIE GILL
University of Wisconsin-La Crosse
Cornelia 8406

17 G. B. KNAPP
University of Wisconsin-La Crosse
G. B. Knapp 14897

18 POSING ON THE COMMONWEALTH
University of Wisconsin-La Crosse
Commonwealth 17158

19 FRANK PARGOUD
University of Wisconsin-La Crosse
Frank Pargoud 8386

20 GEORGE W. WYLLY
University of Wisconsin-La Crosse
George W. Wylly 13611

21 ALEX MITCHELL
University of Wisconsin-La Crosse
Alex Mitchell 9839

22 ADDIE JOHNSTON
University of Wisconsin-La Crosse
Addie Johnston 3804

23 ABNER GILE DECKHANDS
University of Wisconsin-La Crosse
Abner Gile 853

24 GREAT REPUBLIC
University of Wisconsin-La Crosse
Great Republic 22535

25 **GREAT REPUBLIC INTERIOR**
University of Wisconsin-La Crosse
Great Republic 41689

26 **ALEX MITCHELL, 1870s**
University of Wisconsin-La Crosse
Alex Mitchell 6726

27 **ERA NO. 10**
University of Wisconsin-La Crosse
Era No. 10 7272

28 **COMPLETING THE EADS BRIDGE, 1874**
Library of Congress
LC-USZ62-69757

29 **CONS MILLAR**
University of Wisconsin-La Crosse
Cons Millar 8733

30 **ED RICHARDSON**
University of Wisconsin-La Crosse
Ed Richardson 9718

32 **NINE STEAMBOATS AT VICKSBURG**
University of Wisconsin-La Crosse
Clara S. 30372

33 **STEAMBOATS WITH BARRELS AT SUGAR LANDING DOCK**
University of Wisconsin-La Crosse
Clinton 8060

34 **ED RICHARDSON PARLOR**
University of Wisconsin-La Crosse
Ed Richardson 43198

35 **DEAN ADAMS LOADING COTTON**
University of Wisconsin-La Crosse
Dean Adams 8166

36 **BOYS SWIMMING BY F. C. A. DENKMANN**
University of Wisconsin-La Crosse
F. C. A. Denkmann 2500

37 **EDWARD J. GAY**
University of Wisconsin-La Crosse
Edward J. Gay 30683

38 **ECLIPSE IN CASSVILLE, WISCONSIN**
University of Wisconsin-La Crosse
Eclipse 13801

39 **WAGONS PICKING UP CARGO FROM EDWARD J. GAY**
University of Wisconsin-La Crosse
Edward J. Gay 11285

40 **GAMBLING ABOARD THE DORA**
University of Wisconsin-La Crosse
Dora 10375

41 **GOLDEN GATE AT LOUISVILLE**
University of Wisconsin-La Crosse
Golden Gate 813

42 **GEM CITY CREW**
University of Wisconsin-La Crosse
Gem City 06549

43 **E. W. COLE TIED UP**
University of Wisconsin-La Crosse
E. W. Cole 48341

44 **CITY OF VICKSBURG PARLOR**
University of Wisconsin-La Crosse
City of Vicksburg 8227

45 **CROWDED ABNER GILE**
University of Wisconsin-La Crosse
Abner Gile 808

46 **FASHIONABLE WOMEN ON CITY OF WINONA**
University of Wisconsin-La Crosse
City of Winona 5769

47 **DINING IN CITY OF WINONA PARLOR**
University of Wisconsin-La Crosse
City of Winona 03827

48 **FIRST CITY OF ST. LOUIS, 1891**
University of Wisconsin-La Crosse
City of St. Louis(A) 03754

50 **NATCHEZ, GARLAND, AND UNIDENTIFIED BOAT**
University of Wisconsin-La Crosse
Garland 06435

51 **LAST OF TEN GREY EAGLES**
University of Wisconsin-La Crosse
Grey Eagle (C)14465

52 **WOMAN AND CHILDREN BOARDING ELOISE**
University of Wisconsin-La Crosse
Eloise 16077

53 **DUBUQUE PARLOR**
University of Wisconsin-La Crosse
Dubuque 46168

54 **FERD HEROLD, J. N. HARBIN, AND KATE ADAMS**
University of Wisconsin-La Crosse
Ferd Herold 13305

55 **CITY OF QUINCY**
University of Wisconsin-La Crosse
City of Quincy 03549

56 **E. RUTLEDGE TOWING BARGE**
University of Wisconsin-La Crosse
E. Rutledge 06045

57 **A. L. MASON**
University of Wisconsin-La Crosse
A. L. Mason 29185

58 **CITY OF ST. LOUIS WAIT STAFF**
University of Wisconsin-La Crosse
City of St. Louis(A) 8226

59 **DISEMBARKING FROM CITY OF PROVIDENCE**
University of Wisconsin-La Crosse
City of Providence 13171

60 **POSING IN CITY OF PROVIDENCE CABIN**
University of Wisconsin-La Crosse
City of Providence 8519

61 **JOSIE SIVLEY, COLUMBIA, AND INDEPENDENCE**
University of Wisconsin-La Crosse
Columbia(J) 8104

62 **LAST OF TEN GREY EAGLES, NO. 2**
University of Wisconsin-La Crosse
Grey Eagle(C) 44647

Glossary of Steamboat Terms

Like any other field, steamboating generated its own, often-colorful, vocabulary. Terms used during the Steamboat Era and even today may not be easily understood by contemporary readers without explanation. This handy glossary features steamboat-related terms, most of which appear in the text. For more steamboat-related terms and information, visit the online glossary at the Steamboats.com Web site at http://www.steamboats.org/history-education/glossary.html.

—D.M.S.

Aft: A general term referring to the rear section of a boat or ship (see also *stern*).

Bar (or sandbar): A naturally occurring shallow area in or adjacent to a river's channel, composed of sand or sometimes gravel. In very low water, bars may be exposed above the surface. Boats failing to detect bars in time often run aground on them.

Barge: A large, flat-bottomed boat, built mainly for river and canal transport of heavy goods. Most barges are not self-propelled and need to be towed (pushed or pulled) by tugboats or towboats.

Bow: A nautical term that refers to the forward part of the hull of a ship or boat; the point that is most forward when the vessel is underway (see also *fore*).

Boiler: The enclosed iron cylinder in which water was heated to create the steam needed to power a steamboat.

Cabin: On a packet, the long hallway running the length of the interior of the passenger quarters on the boiler deck. Also known as the main cabin or parlor, it served as both the social hall and dining room for the cabin passengers. On either side of the cabin were rows of stateroom doors. On a towboat the cabin was the space aft the officers' rooms on the boiler deck, basically used as a lounging area.

Cabin boy: A low-ranking employee, usually a young boy but not always a minor, who waits on the officers and passengers of a ship, especially running errands for the captain.

Calliope: A steam-powered keyboard instrument usually mounted on the upper deck of a steamboat. Steam is fed into hollow metal pipes of varying lengths to create the sound. Patented in October 1855 by Joshua C. Stoddard, it was initially used by circuses to draw people to their shows or entertain them once they arrived. Showboats, and later excursion boats, took their cue from them and began featuring them in the same manner, to attract and entertain.

Canal: A man-made waterway that allows ships and boats to bypass rapids or falls along a river, or to shorten the distance between two points on a waterway. Before the development of excavation machinery, canals were dug by hand with shovels by large groups of laborers.

Capsized: When a boat or ship is tipped over until disabled. The act of reversing a capsized vessel is called righting.

Capstan: A metal spool for winding up a rope. Placed upright on the deck, the capstan may be revolved manually or mechanically. Early in the Steamboat Era they were turned by hand, but in later years, most boats utilized steam-powered capstans.

Composite hull: A hull design begun in the late 1880s in which the framing and, usually, the sides were built of iron or steel while the bottom was made of wood. This became the transition from all-wood to all-steel hulls.

Deckhand: On a packet which carried an African-American deck crew, the "boss man" (another African-American) on the watch was called the deckhand. He was the go-between for the mate and the roustabouts. On a towboat, a deckhand is a man employed to do deck work and handle mooring lines.

Decommission: The act of officially taking a boat out of service; removing it from the rolls of active vessels on the official government steamboat registry.

Dike: Similar to a levee (see *levee*). An earthen or concrete structure built high along a river to contain the river within its course and help prevent flooding. On the Ohio River before locks and dams were built, dikes were a method of channel improvement. They consisted largely of ridding the snags and constructing long wing dams to funnel the water during drought times into a navigable channel. On the Mississippi, dikes were man-made outcroppings built into the water to protect landing facilities and riverfront buildings.

Draft: The depth of a boat's hull under the waterline. Draft was measured at the bow and stern and could be manipulated by shifting the cargo load fore and aft.

Draw: The section of a drawbridge that opens wide enough or high enough to allow waterborne vessels to pass through. A draw could be a "swing" type, a vertical lift that went straight up evenly, or one that lifted from only one side. Draw is also a nautical term referring to the specific depth of water a vessel needs in order to float.

Dredge: A scooping device for scraping or sucking sediment from the riverbed in order to deepen the navigation channel. A dredger is a ship or boat equipped with a dredge.

Drydock: A narrow basin or vessel that can be flooded to allow a boat to be floated in, then drained to allow that boat to come to rest on a dry platform. Drydocks are used for construction, maintenance, and repair of ships, boats, and other watercraft.

Engineer: The shipboard crew member who operates the engines on a boat or ship. Vessels usually carried more than one engineer so that they could operate in shifts, allowing time for meals and sleep, and ensuring that the engine room was constantly staffed.

Engine room: Where the boat's main engines, generators, compressors, pumps, fuel-lubrication oil purifiers, and other major machinery are located. It is sometimes referred to as the "machinery space."

Excursion boat: A boat that carries passengers only (no freight), mainly for sightseeing or pleasure cruises of short duration. Many excursion boats did not provide staterooms for overnight accommodations.

Excursions (or day cruises): A boat trip taken by individuals or a group of people, usually for leisure or educational purposes. Excursions can be either general admission to the public or chartered by a group of individuals for their private use. Some excursions can be longer than just a single day.

Fathom: A nautical measure of water depth. Six feet equals one fathom.

Fireman: A steamboat crew member employed to tend (stoke) fires under the boilers to ensure a steady flow of heat and steam needed to power the boat.

Fore: The front portion of a boat or ship; the opposite of aft (see also *bow*).

Foundered: When a ship fills with water and sinks. The term is sometimes loosely used to describe a shipwreck, but most often it refers to a ship filling with water after a wreck or a serious hull leak.

Gangplank: A board or set of boards used to construct a temporary means of passage from boat to shore, or from one boat to another. A gangway is a more permanent passageway for the convenience of passengers or the conveyance of freight on shipboard.

Gunboat: A boat carrying one or more long-range deck guns for military purposes. During the Civil War, many packet boats were pressed into service by the armed forces of both the Union and the Confederacy and converted into gunboats. Sometimes, for added protection, they secured metal plates to their exteriors (see *tinclads*). They traveled along major rivers and harbors, helping lay siege to cities and towns along those waterways or attacking other gunboats and enemy vessels.

Harbor boat: A workboat or towboat that worked solely in or around the port area of a river city, performing heavy-duty waterborne tasks in service of that city's port governing body.

Hog chain: A system of chains and steel rods designed to support the weight of the paddle wheel(s) and other heavy onboard structures and prevent wooden hulls from sagging, or "hogging," under heavy loads. The hull construction of western steamboats tended to warp up in the middle and sag at the extremities. Hog chains extended from the forward hull up and over the hurricane deck, and back down to the stern. They could be tightened or loosened as needed by turnbuckles. Some wooden hulled stern-wheelers required several sets of hog chains throughout the vessel for structural support.

Home port (or hailing port): The port of origin for a particular boat, as shown on its registration documents and often lettered on the stern of the ship's hull, on the paddleboxes, or elsewhere on the boat's exterior. In the cruise industry, the term "home port" is often mistakenly used in reference to a ship's port of departure.

Hull: The watertight lower body of a ship or boat. Above the hull comes the superstructure and deckhouse. The line where the hull meets the water surface is called the waterline.

Jetty: A long, slender but sturdy man-made outcropping designed to deepen a navigational channel by narrowing the channel and speeding up the flow of a river. This allows the swifter current to move large amounts of silt and sediment out of the path of waterborne vessels. The Eads Jetties at the mouths of the Mississippi are the best example of this.

Landing barge (or landing boat): A barge permanently moored to the shore and used as a dock or landing for a boat's passengers and/or cargo. It could also be a combination office and storage area for boat companies (with or without living quarters) that was permanently secured to the shore. Hulls of retired steamboats or barges were often reconditioned and re-adapted for this purpose.

Launch: A heavy open or half-decked boat propelled by oars or by an engine.

Levee: To rivermen this term means a sloping or graded wharf of almost any sort. On the Mississippi and other rivers, levees are man-made, built-up embankments along the river to contain the river within its present course and prevent flooding during high water times (similar to a dike).

Lighthouse tender: A ship specifically designed to maintain, support, or tend to staffed lighthouses or lightvessels. They provided supplies, fuel, mail, and transportation for lighthouse personnel to and from shore.

Lock: A chamber built along one side of a river dam for the purpose of raising or lowering the water levels to allow floating traffic to pass the dam.

Lock and dam: A structure that blocks the river during periods of low water to create an artificial pool upstream, combined with facilities for permitting the passage of a boat from one water level to the other.

Low-draft: Water too shallow for a boat or ship to float in.

Maiden voyage: The first journey made by a boat or ship after a "shakedown cruise" to ensure that everything is functioning correctly.

Master: The highest-ranking officer on a boat; often called the captain or commander. Master may also refer to the degree of navigational proficiency attained by a boat's captain, sometimes determined through testing by government maritime regulatory agencies.

Moored: Tied to a dock or wharf or to some point on the shore by strong, thick ropes called mooring lines. May also refer to a vessel that is at anchor away from the shore (anchorage).

Mothballed: A term used to describe a moored boat not presently in active service, but is not officially off the registry and can be reactivated at any time it is felt necessary.

Packet: Refers to the type of steam-powered vessels that dominated America's river systems in the 1800s and early 1900s. Packet boats were designed to transport people and commerce on the larger rivers and featured overnight accommodations, meals, and other amenities. The first packet boat was built in 1811. The last true packet boats were built during the first decade of the twentieth century. By the 1930s the packet steamboat was practically extinct.

Paddlebox: The covering, usually made of wood, over the paddle wheels of side-wheeler boats. Side-wheels were enclosed mainly to prevent spray from blowing onto the boats' passengers. The names of the boats and their cities of origin or home port were often displayed on the paddleboxes.

Pilothouse: The room on a steamboat that contained the wheel that steered the vessel and accommodated the ship's pilot or captain who controlled the wheel and other navigational details. Early steamboats had their pilothouses on deck level, and later models elevated them above the main deck for greater visibility by their pilots.

Port: The left side of the boat or ship facing the front of the vessel (opposite of starboard). A port is also a city along a navigable river having adequate docking facilities and from which a large amount of commerce, both passenger and freight, is handled.

Propeller: A type of fan that transmits power by converting rotational motion into thrust. It can be used to drive a ship or the fluid within a pump. It consists of one or more blades around a central shaft and operates like a rotating screw or wing (see also *screw propeller*).

Propeller towboat: A towboat that moves under the power of a propeller rather than a paddle wheel.

Purser: An officer on a ship who handles financial accounts and various documents relating to the ship and who ensures the safekeeping of money and valuables for passengers.

Rafter: A workboat that pushed rafts of logs to sawmills along the rivers, especially along the upper Mississippi. Some rafters doubled as passenger carriers and excursion boats.

Raft: In steamboat terminology, a large group of logs bound together and pulled or pushed by a rafter to a sawmill. In general terminology, any flat floating structure used for travel over water. It is the most basic boat design, characterized by the absence of a hull. Instead, rafts are kept afloat using any combination of buoyant materials such as wood, sealed barrels, or inflated air chambers.

Railroad transfer boat: A large workboat that operated as a ferry for railroads. In the absence of bridges, railroad transfer boats carried train engines and their cars from a railhead on one side of a river to a railhead on the opposite side.

Rip rap (or riprap): Material such as discarded construction elements, concrete chunks, building rubble, rocks, or other sturdy materials used to armor shorelines, streambeds, bridge abutments, pilings, and other shoreline structures against scour, water, or ice erosion.

Roustabouts: Men employed to work under the mate on the deck of a packet. The term usually referred to African-Americans but later went into general usage to describe those who performed the hard, physical "dirty work" aboard a vessel.

Screw propeller: A propeller that was much smaller than a paddle wheel, featuring rotating blades that churned the water and moved a vessel forward (or backward if the blades were set in reverse). It was a later development in maritime technology that was usually placed at the rear underside of a boat rather than as an exterior appendage like a paddle wheel.

Showboat: A floating theater built solely for the entertainment of passengers. Constructed like a huge box on a barge, it was usually provided with a box office, seats, a stage, scenery, and all of the accoutrements of a land-based theater and offered legitimate stage attractions.

Side-wheeler: A steamboat with two paddle wheels, one on either side of the boat. In all but the smallest side-wheelers, the paddle wheel was enclosed in a housing (paddlebox) to minimize spray. Side-wheels operated independently of each other through separate furnaces and boiler systems, thus allowing boats to turn and maneuver more easily.

Skiff: A small boat or yawl often carried aboard larger vessels to transport one to four people from ship to shore. Early skiffs were powered manually by oars; later models by gas- or diesel-driven propeller engines.

Snag: A large, heavy object embedded in a river that created an obstruction or hazard to navigation. The term most often applied to trees and thick limbs encountered singularly or in clusters. Snags hidden just below the surface of the water could tear a hole in the wooden hull of a boat, causing it to take on water and sink.

Snagboat: A shallow-draft, double-hulled steamboat designed to remove snags from the river channel. Removal usually was accomplished by pulling or lifting the snag from its location and then cutting it into small sections.

Sponson: A structure projecting from the side or main deck of a vessel to support a gun or the outer edge of a paddlebox. Can also refer to a buoyant appendage at the gunwale of a canoe to resist capsizing.

Starboard: The right side of the boat or ship facing the front of the vessel (opposite of port side).

Stateroom: Sleeping rooms located on either side of the cabin. Most staterooms were small with nothing more in them than a bunk bed and a washstand and chair. The term supposedly is derived from the tradition of naming each room after a U.S. state rather than assigning a number to it.

Steam whistle: A steam-powered device fashioned from metal pipes and mounted on the deck of steamboats to warn approaching vessels of their proximity or to signal bridgetenders to open drawbridges for their passage. Steam whistles were also sounded when boats approached river landings to announce their arrival and just before departures as a "last call" to alert late arrivers that they're about to embark.

Stern: The rear or aft part of a ship or boat, technically defined as the area built up over the sternpost, extending upward. It lies opposite of the bow, the foremost part of a ship.

Stern-wheeler: A steamboat with one large paddle wheel located at the stern.

Striker: An apprentice pilot. The more commonly used term is cub pilot.

Survey boat: A ship designed and equipped to carry out marine research, such as water depth and current speed. Research roles performed by these vessels can either be combined into a single vessel or assigned to a vessel dedicated to a singular purpose.

Texas (upper) deck: A long, narrow cabin located on top of the skylight roof of a packet boat and surmounted by the pilothouse. This deck usually contained the staterooms for the captain and boat crew. It got its name because it was a new type of deck that was being added to many steamboats at the same time the state of Texas was being added to the United States.

Tinclad: A gunboat armored with plates of thin iron that resemble tin to help repel light enemy fire. The plates only covered the pilothouse, engines, and boilers, but not the rest of the boat. They were commonly used to land troops and supplies and were usually kept at a safe distance from heavy fire. They were better protected than woodclads, which were only shielded by thick wood, but less protected than ironclads, which required heavier armor and were often the lead boats in a river assault.

Tow: One or more barges or other floating vessels a self-propelled vessel is transporting from one location to another. A tow is made up when it has been hitched together and prepared for moving. A barge moored to the front of a towing steamer is the tow barge and the ones out in front are the lead barges. When a barge is towed alongside a towboat it is "slung under her arm." When pulled behind, as is sometimes done in times of floating ice, the barges are said to be "railroaded."

Tramp: A boat or ship engaged in the tramp trade is one which does not have a fixed schedule or published ports of call. Steamboats that engaged in the tramp trade were sometimes called tramp steamers, tramp freighters, or trampers.

Turned turtle: A colloquialism used to describe a boat that has capsized and turned upside-down in the water with the bottom of the hull facing upward, like a turtle on its back.

Watchmen: Crew members who monitored a boat's activity, usually at night when most of the crew was sleeping. Watchmen were trained to spot unusual or potentially dangerous activity on the vessel such as fires, navigational hazards, and malfunctioning parts or equipment.

Ways: When a boat was pulled out of the water for repairs, it was said to be "out on the ways."

Workboats: Steamboats designed and built to perform waterborne tasks. They generally did not take on passengers other than those employed to work aboard the boat.

Yard ferryboat: A packet or workboat pressed into service by a port or harbor governing authority or the U.S. armed forces to transport personnel and equipment across waterways or from the shore to points offshore and back.

BIBLIOGRAPHY

BOOKS

Davis, William C. *Portraits of the Riverboats*. San Diego: Thunder Bay Press, 2001.

Drago, Harry Sinclair. *The Steamboaters: From the Early Side-Wheelers to the Big Packets*. New York: Dodd, Mead & Company, 1967.

Gandy, Thomas H. and Joan W. Gandy. *The Mississippi Steamboat Era in Historic Photographs: Natchez to New Orleans 1870-1920*. New York: Dover Publications, 1987.

O'Neil, Paul. *The Rivermen*. New York: Time-Life Books, 1975.

Sheffer, H. R. *Paddle wheelers*. Mankato, MN: Crestwood House, 1982.

Way, Frederick Jr. *Way's Packet Directory 1848-1983: Passenger Steamboats of the Mississippi River System Since the Advent of Photography in Mid-Continent America*. Athens, Ohio: Ohio University Press, 1983.

Way, Frederick Jr. *Way's Steam Towboat Directory*. Athens, Ohio: Ohio University Press, 1990.

UNPUBLISHED STUDIES

Clay, Floyd M. "History of Navigation on the Lower Mississippi." National Waterways Study for the U.S. Army Engineer Water Resources Support Center, Institute for Water Resources. 1983.

WEB SITES

www.steamboats.com

www.steamboats.org

Dr. V. Fred Rayser, "Ghosts of the Mississippi River," *Fate Magazine*, October 1, 2000. *Llewellyn's Article Archive*. Llewellyn Worldwide, Ltd.: Woodbury, MN. http://www.llewellyn.com/bookstore/article.php?id=49.

HISTORIC PHOTOS OF
STEAMBOATS
ON THE MISSISSIPPI

From the earliest rudimentary conveyances to the floating palaces of the present day, a period of 200 years, steamboats have carved out a very special place in American history, especially along the Mississippi River and its tributaries, where they brought passengers, cargo, mail, entertainment, and news—both good and bad—to the settlements of a still-developing nation.

With paddle-wheels churning, tall smokestacks billowing, calliopes singing, and steam whistles sounding, the steamboats of the Mighty Mississippi proudly ruled the river. Some offered all the comforts of home (and more); others did the work for the industries that transformed the United States into the industrial giant it became. They carried presidents and kings, socialites and commoners, cotton and coal, lumber and steel. They enabled some of our nation's major cities to grow and flourish.

Told through historic photographs in these pages, the story of steamboats that plied the Mississippi and the glorious era they symbolized is vividly captured and enshrined for generations to come.

Dean M. Shapiro grew up near the Hudson River in New York where some of the first commercial steamboats ran. He now lives in Gretna, Louisiana, across the Mississippi River from New Orleans, where excursion steamboats still run, and within earshot of the *Natchez* calliope. He graduated from Ramapo College of New Jersey with a B.A. in history and is the author of four other books, one of which became a made-for-TV movie *(Prophet of Evil: The Ervil LeBaron Story)* that aired on CBS in 1993. A journalist and freelance writer for 40 years, he has more than 1,500 published articles in newspapers, magazines, and Web sites to his credit. He currently writes for the New Orleans Tourism Marketing Corporation's Web site and monthly newsletter, *TravelHost* magazine, *Where Y'At* magazine, NewOrleans.com, and *Arthur Hardy's Mardi Gras Guide.* He is also a writer for world-renowned health and fitness guru, Mackie Shilstone.

WWW.TURNERPUBLISHING.COM

www.ingramcontent.com/pod-product-compliance
Lightning Source LLC
Chambersburg PA
CBHW061227150426
42812CB00054BA/2537